Time *to* Weave

Simply elegant projects
to make in almost no time

Jane Patrick

INTERWEAVE PRESS

Text and process photography © 2006 by Jane Patrick
Photography: Joe Coca
Cover and interior design: Susan Wasinger

INTERWEAVE PRESS

201 East Fourth Street
Loveland, CO 80537-5655 USA
www.interweave.com

Printed and bound in China by Pimlico Book International

Library of Congress Cataloging-in-Publication Data

Patrick, Jane.
  Time to weave : simply elegant projects to make in almost no time /
Jane Patrick, author.
      p. cm.
  Includes bibliographical references and index.
  ISBN 13: 978-1-931499-59-0 (pbk.)
  ISBN 10: 1-931499-59-4 (pbk.)
  1. Hand weaving. I. Title.
  TT848.P4 2006
  746.42—dc22

                        2006007125

10 9 8 7 6 5 4 3 2 1

Fyrir Húsmæðraskólann á Löngumýri...

THANK YOU TO THE FOLLOWING PEOPLE FOR MAKING THIS PROJECT POSSIBLE.

To Interweave Press for inviting me to write a book.

To my editors: Linda Ligon for her guidance and encouragement and Ann Budd for good technical editing and thoughtful suggestions.

To Susan Wasinger for a superb book design and Paulette Livers for putting it all together.

To Joe Coca, for masterful pictures, photo consultation, as well as technical support.

Thanks to McGuckin Hardware for an amazing selection and knowledgeable personnel who were always at the ready to help me find what I needed. Thanks to my local yarn store, Shuttles, Spindles, and Skeins, for helpfulness and a vast inventory of ready materials. In addition, I am grateful to the Boulder Public Library and Handweavers Guild of Boulder for their great collections of textile books that were helpful in researching numerous techniques in this book.

Thank you to Cotton Clouds, Crystal Palace Yarns, and Harrisville Designs for supplying yarn.

To my colleagues in the office at Schacht: Betsy Blumenthal, Gail Matthews, Suzanne Najarian, Sarah Nelson, and Rick Santala, who kept it all going while I was otherwise engrossed in this project. To my intern Jessica Knickman for lending a much needed helping hand, as well as superb ideas. (Thanks to KCAI for sending her to me just when I needed her.)

To my friends and sewing experts Louise Bradley and Mary Kay Stoehr.

To Fun Club for monthly escapes and moral support.

To my sisters Judy and Sarah and daughter Nora who knew I could do it.

And finally, to my hubby, Barry Schacht, my best critic and enthusiastic supporter.

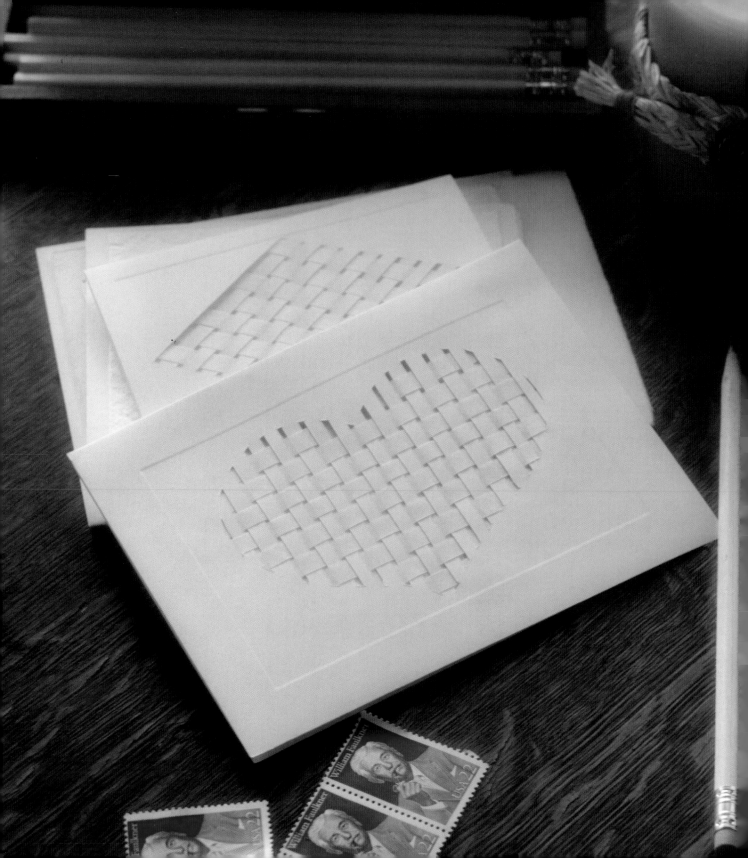

Time *to* Weave

CONTENTS

INTRODUCTION

Creating an object with your own hands is about more than a finished project. Making something is repeated motions, little decisions, taking command of materials to form them into a new existence. In the doing there is also quiet, time to think and reflect. Often, you'll find new ideas or solutions to life's problems. You gain a deep satisfaction from making something by hand. The object becomes more than itself, because it was created by you.

In 1972, when I peeked into the weaving studio of the home ec school at Löngumýri, Iceland, and saw a room full of looms, I knew weaving was something I must do. A few years later, weaving had become central to my life, influencing how I spent my time and how I viewed the world. Lately, I've realized that weaving has given me what many search a lifetime to find: a passion and a place to be.

Weaving is a prism that colors the world I live in. I see the world in terms of its hues and textures and shapes. Weaving binds me to those who have gone before and those who continue to make cloth for work or pleasure. Weaving has been my livelihood, first as editor of Handwoven magazine and currently as sales manager for Schacht Spindle Company. It has also been my hobby: it's what I do for fun. Because of weaving I've found lifelong friends—and even my husband, whom I met one day at my local weaving shop. Weaving has provided countless creative hours that can be all consuming. It is this passion and love of weaving that I hope will infuse the pages of this book and lead you on a path of discovery. Your world will never again quite be the same.

Tile wrap begins on page 58.

WEAVING BASICS

In weaving, two sets of elements—threads, yarns, paper strips, or pliable sticks, for instance—are interlaced. One set, the warp, is crossed by another, the weft. Together, warp and weft form a woven structure. The simplest weave, plain weave, is a simple over-under, over-under pattern. From this simple basis infinite variations are possible.

Weaving can be done without a loom, as in basket weaving, or with a loom, as in fabric weaving. In either case, weaving is the same: sets of two elements crossing each other.

A loom is simply a device that holds the warp elements in place and taut so that the weft can be woven over and under across them. A loom can be as simple as a picture frame or piece of cardboard, or as sophisticated as a computer-controlled machine. No matter the style or degree of sophistication, a loom's primary function is to hold the warp. The main difference between a simple frame loom and a complex loom is the amount of work it will do for you.

All the projects in this book can be woven either without a loom or on a simple frame. The following discussion applies to projects woven on looms.

The first step in weaving is to put the warp on the loom—a process called warping. In this book, the warp is placed directly on the loom or frame. (More sophisticated looms require many more preparatory steps.)

As stated earlier, weaving consists of two sets of threads: warp and weft. Individual warp threads are referred to as warp ends, ends,

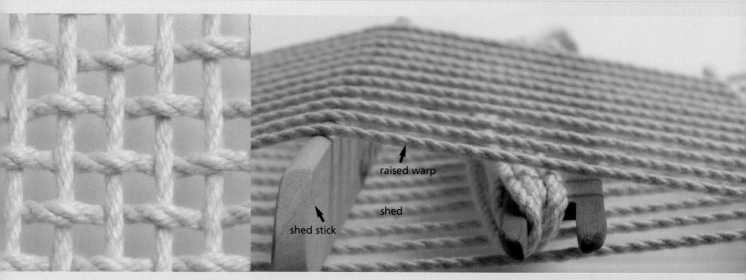

Woven fabric. The most basic of weaves, plain weave, is a simple over-under, over-under interlacement.

The space between raised and lowered warp threads is called the shed.

raised warp

shed

shed stick

or threads. The weft is the set of threads that cross the warp. Each line of weft is called a pick or shot. If the weft is yarn, thread, rag strips, or other long, flexible material, it is usually wound onto a shuttle for easy handling. The kind of shuttle I've generally used is a simple stick shuttle.

You can pass the weft over and under alternate warp threads one at a time or you can lift alternate warp threads all at once to make a space for passing the shuttle through. This space is called the shed. A shed stick (or pick-up stick), a flat stick with pointy ends, is often inserted in the shed to hold it open for the shuttle to pass through. The edge of the weaving where the shuttle exits and then re-enters to return to the other side is called the selvedge. The fell line is the last row of weft you've woven in the developing cloth—the place where woven and unwoven warp meet.

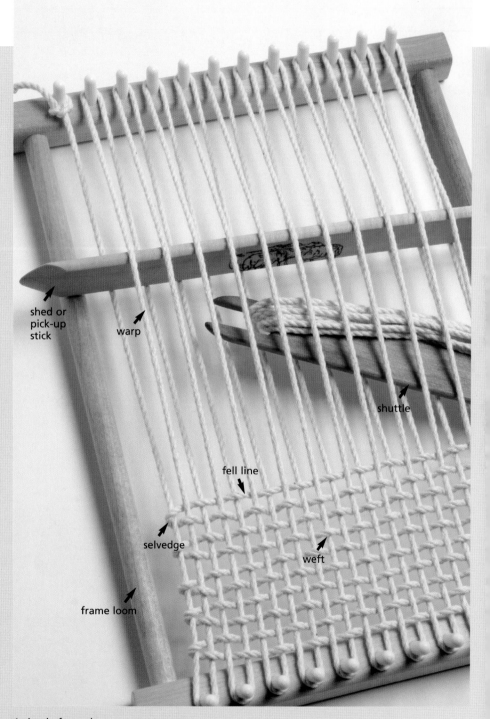

A simple frame loom.

A FEW OF MY FAVORITE THINGS

These tools and materials have been helpful to me in making the projects in this book. I've found them, if not indispensable, handy in speeding and simplifying many tasks.

CUTTING MAT, QUILTER'S RULE, AND ROTARY CUTTER

You can find these items in most fabric and craft stores. A cutting mat generally has a grid marked in ⅛" (3 mm) sections. I use it to help cut strips, eliminating the need to measure and mark before cutting. I also use the grid as a guide when weaving flat elements, such as for the cork mat, the first project in this book. Get the biggest cutting mat you can afford and have room for.

Since I discovered the rotary cutter, I use it whenever possible. It is quick and makes an excellent straight cut. A note of caution when using a rotary cutter: never hurry and always pay attention when cutting, as the blade is razor sharp—one of the reasons it works so well. Also, to avoid mishaps, retract the blade when not in use.

A clear, gridded quilter's rule is useful as a cutting guide and for use with the rotary cutter. I like the way it keeps my hands away from that sharp blade.

OTHER CUTTING TOOLS

A pair of large scissors with 4" (10 cm) blades are a good all-purpose cutting tool. Additionally, I use cuticle scissors with curved blades for trimming yarns and threads. Because the blades are curved, they point away from the surface I am cutting, preventing errant snips. Utility or mat knives are excellent for cutting thick materials, such as the carpet runner and cork used for projects in this book. An Exacto knife is also handy for cutting jobs where you need to start and stop at an exact point.

From left to right: cutting mat, quilter's rule, rotary cutter.

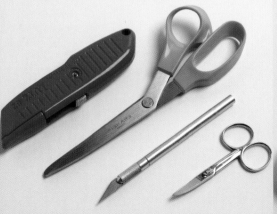

Cutting tools, left to right: mat knife, scissors with 4" (10 cm) blades, Exacto knife, cuticle scissors.

Measuring tools from left to right: tape measure, sewing gauge, T-square.

MEASURING TOOLS

A T-square is handy for aligning a piece of fabric or paper prior to cutting. I use a sewing gauge often when I need to measure short, equal increments. And no work room is complete without a tape measure.

OTHER HANDY TOOLS

I make liberal use of masking tape, which is terrific for temporarily securing materials together or for anchoring them on the table for working. Sometimes I use masking tape on the ends of string or yarn to prevent fraying. I use it on the edges of cork when cutting it to prevent it from cracking and splaying out. Masking tape has holding power but is easy to remove.

For braiding, I use duct tape to tape the ends of my yarns to my working surface.

I use a variety of weights to hold pieces in place or to weigh down anything that wants to curve, like paper or reed. I have some smooth, heavy rocks I've gathered from various trips and love using these for smaller jobs—they are both pleasing to the eye and touch and pleasant reminders of vacations with friends and family.

The weight I use most often is an ordinary brick. To protect my work and table, I wrapped the brick in a scrap of fleece. (A friend improved my idea by stitching the fabric around the brick—a permanent solution to a makeshift idea.)

I keep a basket of spring-style clothespins handy and use them often, especially for basket weaving. They are cheap and readily available.

I have been collecting stuff for years, most of it without an intended use. Collecting can lead to unwanted clutter, not to mention a storage nightmare. The trick is to organize it so that when you do decide that the shells you collected ten years ago are just right for your current project, you can actually lay your hands on them! I like to store small items, such as buttons, in plastic storage drawers often used for hardware. Large projects and yarns are stored in big plastic see-through stackable bins. If you must use cardboard boxes for storage, take the time to label the box with detailed descriptions as you pack the materials away. It will be time well spent. (I've learned this one the hard way—nothing is more frustrating than to know you have the perfect yarn or trim but being unable to find it.)

Other favorite things, from left to right: clothespins, masking tape, fabric wrapped brick weight, plastic storage bin, rock weights.

Choosing appropriate materials is one of the challenges of designing a project for a specific use. For this mat, I wanted a material that would protect the table from hot pots, yet be attractive enough to use at dinnertime. Cork, a nonconducting, cushy material that is resistant to molds and mildew, as well as being flame retardant, fit the specifications I was looking for.

A renewable resource, cork is harvested from the outer bark of the cork oak tree (*Quercus suber L.*) without damaging the tree. Historically cork has been used for sandal soles, storage vessels, and fishing net floats. Today cork is primarily used for wine stoppers. This project uses cork sheeting, a by-product of the bottle-stopper industry, made of waste bits that are ground up and formed into sheets with adhesive.

> *"There is nothing in a caterpillar that tells you it's going to be a butterfly."*
>
> —*Buckminster Fuller*

OVERVIEW: Basic over-under, over-under plain weave is used for this cork mat. I've given this *simplest of structures* a different look by simply alternating thick and thin horizontal, or weft, strips. I cut the strips from cork sheeting sold in hardware and craft stores. Assembly is *easy as pie:* just lay down the verticals, or warp, and weave over and under horizontally with the weft. To help *keep all the elements evenly spaced,* I used the grid on a cutting mat as a template.

INSTRUCTIONS

MATERIALS AND EQUIPMENT

Cork sheet measuring ⅛ x 12 x 22" (.3 x 30.5 x 56 cm); pencil; cutting mat; mat or utility knife; straight edge; masking tape; plastic wrap; glue; glue gun; toothpicks.

RESOURCES

Cork sheets are available at craft and hardware stores.

FINISHED SIZE

About 11½ x 11" (29 x 28 cm).

HINTS:

+ To prevent the cork from splaying out and tearing at the edges when cutting, tape the cork strips to the cutting board with masking tape.

+ Use a weight to anchor the weaving on the cutting board to prevent the weaving from moving around.

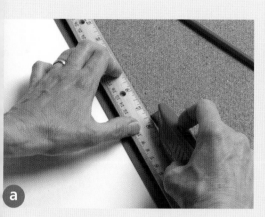

a

b

c

1 Cut 13 strips, each measuring 1 x 12" (2.5 x 30.5 cm) and 7 strips, each measuring ⅜ x 12" (1 x 30.5 cm). Using a marked cutting mat as a measuring guide, mark off the widths with a pencil. With mat knife and straight edge, cut strips for weaving (see figure a).

2 Use the cutting mat as your weaving guide. (To protect the surface from glue, cover the board with plastic wrap.) Place 5 strips vertically (the warp) on the board with a 1" (2.5 cm) space in between each strip. Weave over, under, over, under, alternating 1" and ⅜" (2.5 and 1 cm) wide strips, beginning and ending with 1" (2.5 cm) strips. Snug up the wefts so that there is no space in between the rows (see figure b).

3 Once you have everything in place, use the cutting board grid to adjust the warps and wefts. Check to be sure that there is 1" (2.5 cm) between the warps and that the wefts are even at the edges. Because the wefts are woven tightly, they will not slide around; therefore it is necessary to glue the strips only around the perimeter. I glued the warps first, always checking the position of a strip with the board grid before applying the glue. Place a small dot of glue in the center of the join area. Working quickly, use a toothpick to smooth out the glue (see figure c). Then press the join firmly for a second or two. After the warps are glued down, glue the wefts.

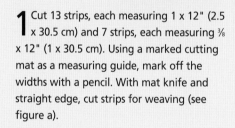

d

4 Trim the warps evenly along the edges using a straight edge and mat knife. Trim any uneven weft edges (see figure d).

VARIATIONS

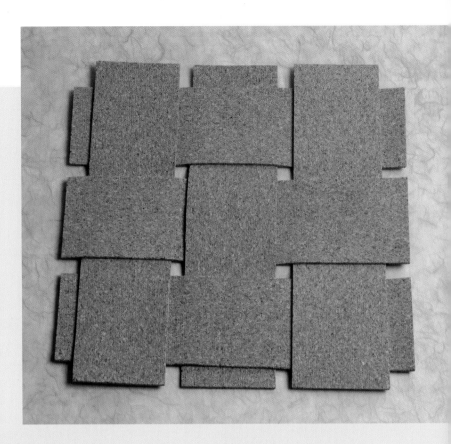

SCALE MAKES A DIFFERENCE

These two mats illustrate how the same plain-weave structure can appear quite different if the size of the elements is varied. For the mat above, just six 3" (7.5 cm) wide cork strips are used to make a chunky, stylized design. In contrast, the mat at the left is woven with 1½" (3.8 cm) wide strips, producing a more casual look.

NEW USE FOR CONSTRUCTION MATERIALS

Cardboard furring strips used for leveling drywall are the weaving material for this decorative mat. Furring strips are precut, dense cardboard slats found wherever building supplies are sold. To prepare the strips for weaving, I laid six of them side by side and sponged them with gradations of orange and yellow paint. I then laid an additional six slats in similar fashion and sponged them with shades of green. Keeping the slats in the same order I painted them, I crossed the orange shades with the greens. For a more durable (though not washable) finish, I sprayed the finished mat with clear acrylic.

FUN FOAM BROOCH

Even your kid's art supplies are not immune to weaving material searches. For this lightweight brooch, measuring just over 2½" (6.5 cm) square, I cut strips of gray, red, and black fun foam and wove them in a plaid. To secure the weaving and embellish the surface, I stitched small seed beads through every intersection. A clasp glued to the back turned my mini-weaving into a brooch.

FURTHER READING

If you realize suddenly that weaving is something you want to do, then I suggest you get connected to the weaving community. The quickest way to become a part of what's going on is to subscribe to a weaving magazine. They are great resources for information, conferences, and supplies. Please refer to the list in the Resources on page 122.

HEARTH RUG

’ve discovered it's important to mull things over when looking for solutions. As I think through ideas, I often turn to books to study how other weavers have solved design problems. You do not need to reinvent the wheel each time.

For this project, I wanted a small rug that could be woven without a loom, be structurally sound and visually appealing, and fairly quick to make. I tried cutting ordinary carpet scraps into strips and weaving them, but the edges frayed too much. Then I found rubber-backed carpet runner at the local hardware store and fell in love with its chunky ribbed texture. The rubber backing kept the strips from fraying as well as providing a nonslip surface.

The next problem was how to secure the strips in place once they were woven. I experimented with spot-gluing the edge pieces—a workable solution, but not very interesting. What textile technique could I use that would prevent the edges from unweaving—and add a little visual accent?

Twining, an ancient technique used in basket and rug making long before anyone thought of inventing a loom, solved all my design problems. Twining has been used to secure the ends of rugs, to make sturdy baskets, and even to construct whole pieces of cloth. If you are familiar with Chilkat blankets of Alaska or taaniko cloth of the New Zealand Maori, then you've seen textiles made with twining.

For this rug, I cut wide strips of carpet runner, wove them in a simple over-under pattern, and secured them with twining in red and black cord. I love that my nontraditional rug design was made possible by a twining technique invented 8,000 years ago.

OVERVIEW: Rubber-backed runner carpet is cut into strips and *woven in a simple over-under pattern* for this hearth rug. The rugged, densely *textured strips are accented* with red and black braided cord twining. Here, the red cord shows on the surface only where it wraps around the black cords *between each warp.*

INSTRUCTIONS

MATERIALS AND EQUIPMENT

Rubber-backed carpet runner, measuring 27 x 58" (68.5 x 147.5 cm); ¼" (6 mm) wide polyester braided cord, 9 yd (8.25 m) each of red and black; cutting mat; utility or mat knife; straight edge; masking tape; scissors; large crochet hook (I used size P/16 [15 mm]); matches or lighter; safety pins; sewing needle and thread.

RESOURCES

Look for rolls of carpet runners at hardware and carpet stores. This material is often sold by the foot, so you can purchase just what you need. The ¼" (6 mm) braid is sold by the roll or by the length at hardware and camping stores.

FINISHED SIZE

About 19½ x 33" (49.5 x 84 cm).

{*}

HINTS:

+ *Because the rug pieces are quite large, you may find it easiest to work on the floor.*

+ *To keep the cord ends from fraying, singe them with a match or lighter.*

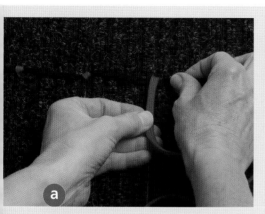

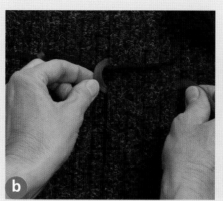

1 Cut 6 strips of carpet runner, each measuring 2½ x 36" (6.5 x 91.5 cm). Cut 10 strips, each measuring 2½ x 21½" (6.5 x 54.5 cm). Using a utility knife, straight edge, and cutting mat, cut on the right side of the runner in between the carpet ribs. Note: The rubber backing grid and the woven ribs of the runner do not line up, so cut on the right side to be sure that you are cutting along the ribs. Your weaving will look much neater if you do.

2 Place the six 36" (91.5 cm) strips (the warps) parallel to each other and about ⅛" (3 mm) apart. To keep the warps from moving around as you start to weave, tape them to your work surface with masking tape. Tie the red and black cords together with an overhand knot, leaving about 6" (15 cm) tails. To manage the lengths of cord better, wrap them into butterflies (see How to Make a Butterfly, page 23). Working 4" (10 cm) from the top edge and beginning on the left side, twine across to the other side in this way (see How to Twine, page 23): place the red cord behind the first carpet strip (or warp), carry the black cord across the top of the first warp (you now have a warp sandwiched between a black cord on the top and a red cord on the bottom). Next, bring the red cord up in the space between the first warp and second warp. If you have trouble grabbing the cord with your fingers, use a crochet hook. Wrap the red cord around the black (see figure a) and return it to the back (see figure b). Pull tight to secure. Work in this way all the way to the other side. You'll notice that the black cord always stays on top. Think of the black cord as the lazy one, with the red cord doing all the work.

3 Weave the first crosswise carpet strip, the weft, over the warps in an over-under, over-under pattern, making sure that you go over the first warp (or strip) on the right. Adjust the weft so that it extends out about equally on either side—about 4" (10 cm). To twine the second row, sandwich the carpet strip just woven so that the black cord is on top and the red is on the bottom and so that they are in position at the right side of your work (see figure c). Twine across to the other side as before.

4 Weave the next carpet strip, going over the strips that you went under on the first row, and vice versa (see figure d). Alternate twining with weaving until all 10 carpet strips are woven, ending with a row of twining.

5 Adjust the strips to make sure everything is even, and then use a sewing needle and thread to stitch the cord ends to themselves on the back (see How to Join the Cords Together, page 23). Trim the carpet strips along the edges to about 2½" (6.5 cm) long.

"What can be more comforting than to turn for a time to something as old and as beautiful as weaving—something that has come down to us through the ages, unhindered by wars and famines, by floods or earthquakes, and forever new under our fingers."
—Mary Atwater,
Byways in Handweaving

TECHNIQUES

JOINING THE CORDS TOGETHER

Wrap the cord with matching sewing thread to prevent raveling. Overlap the cords about 1" (2.5 cm) and stitch them together with the sewing thread. To temporarily secure the ends, you can pin them together with a safety pin.

HOW TO TWINE

In the most basic form of twining, two weft elements cross each other between each warp. The twining technique used for this project is a variation in which one cord stays on the top surface and the other cord comes to the surface between each pair of warps, wraps around the surface cord, and then returns to the back before coming up again in the next space between warps.

HOW TO MAKE A BUTTERFLY

1 Make a figure eight with yarn or cord between your thumb and little finger (see figure a).

2 Wind back and forth several times (see figure b).

3 Remove the yarn or cord from your hand and wrap one end around the middle of the bundle. Tuck in the end to secure it (see figure c). Pull out the other end to use as weft.

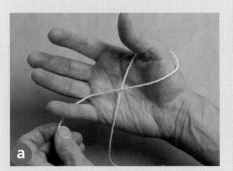

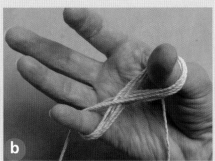

VARIATIONS

Try materials that have different weights, textures, or surfaces.

HOT MAT

The variation below uses thinner rubber-backed carpeting and round woven polyester cord in two colors. I frayed the ends of the cords intentionally to provide design interest.

BLACK-ON-BLACK PLACEMAT

This sturdy mat (right) is a breeze to weave and is finished almost before you know you've begun. Woven with 1½" (3.8 cm) wide polyester strapping, this placemat is simply over-under, over-under, with the weaving kept in place with fabric glue.

BLACK-AND-WHITE COASTER

Black woven polyester strips (purchased at the hardware store) in one direction are crossed with white in the other to weave a checkerboard (below). The perimeter is glued with fabric glue. This is a fast and fun project to make for a housewarming gift.

FURTHER READING

If you decide you really want to weave rugs, then you'll want to get your hands on a copy of Peter Collingwood's *The Techniques of Rug Weaving* (Watson-Guptill Publications, 1970). In this volume, he doggedly explores everything you'll need to know about weaving a solid rug—plus many rug-weaving techniques explored in depth. To pursue rug weaving in earnest, you'll need a sturdy loom and some weaving experience. Taking a class at a shop, art center, or school is a great way to learn to weave. For a list of places to learn to weave, visit these websites: www.spinningandweaving.org; www.interweave.com; and www.weavespindye.org.

To explore twined rugs made on a large frame, read Bobbie Irwin's *Twined Rag Rugs* (Krause Publications, 2000). This in-depth study investigates this rug technique with clear instructions and illustrations, tips, historical anecdotes, and patterns.

've had a love affair with paper for many years. Part of paper's appeal is that it appears to be an ephemeral substance, yet it can have incredible strength—and beauty. I first became aware of this when I attended an exhibition of Chinese crafts some years ago and found myself entirely captivated by the artisans making paper. Repeating over and over in smooth, seamless motions, they dunked their deckles in pulp vats, skimming off just the right amount to produce sheet after sheet of beautiful, creamy paper of a quality I'd never known.

"The whole notion of archaic technology is so interesting. Why is anything
handmade important? Printing on handmade paper . . . gives a joy, a connection with other
people you don't get with a machinemade object. You enjoy fine craftsmanship . . . it enhances
your quality of life on a very sophisticated level."
—Kathryn Clark, Inksmith, Seattle, Washington, 1996 quoted in the
The Book of Fine Paper *by Silvie Turner*

OVERVIEW: Making your own *paper is easy and rewarding,* but it's outside the scope of this book. However, you can bring a touch of *personal creativity* to ready-made note cards by adding woven patterns and motifs. The effect is lovely—and *the technique is easy:* just draw a design on the wrong side of the front, cut slits in the card, *weave across with paper,* and back with a like color. Using good-quality cards will contribute to the elegance of your greeting.

INSTRUCTIONS

MATERIALS AND EQUIPMENT

4½ x 6" (11.5 x 15 cm) white note card with beveled edge; thin off-white paper for weft; stiff white paper for backing; Exacto knife; cutting mat; straight edge; ruler; pencil; glue stick.

RESOURCES

These supplies are sold at paper, card, and stationery stores.

FINISHED SIZE

4½ x 6" (11.5 x 15 cm).

HINTS:

+ Work in the middle of the cutting board, lining up the paper on the grid.

+ The success of the weaving lies in uniform "warps." Therefore, it is important to take care in measuring and cutting.

+ When cutting slippery paper, place a very small piece of masking tape at each corner of the card to keep it in place.

+ A new, sharp blade in your Exacto knife will help make clean cuts.

a

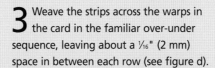

b

c

d

e

1 Draw the design on the wrong side of the card front. Measure and mark lines alternately ¹⁄₁₆" (2 mm) and ³⁄₁₆" (6 mm) apart across the image to be woven (see figure a). Use an Exacto knife to carefully cut out the ¹⁄₁₆" (2 mm) spaces completely to create warps in the card (see figure b).

2 Cut the thin off-white paper into ¼" (6 mm) wide strips (see figure c).

3 Weave the strips across the warps in the card in the familiar over-under sequence, leaving about a ¹⁄₁₆" (2 mm) space in between each row (see figure d).

4 Secure the weaving by gluing down the ends of the woven paper ends with a glue stick (see figure e). Cut a piece of paper to match the card and glue it to the back to cover the raw edges of your weaving.

VARIATIONS

Note: all the projects and examples in this chapter were designed by Jessica Knickman.

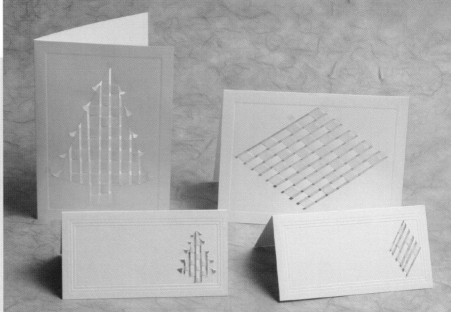

COORDINATED PAPERS

This is a great way to carry out a party theme: weave invitations and place cards with the same design (above). You'll delight your guests and add a special charm to your event.

BUTTERFLY GREETING

This design is all about presentation (above). The small butterfly is cut out of wallpaper and woven with a different printed paper. This small figure might have become lost on the card if it weren't for the layering of first a dense handmade paper, then a strip of botanical paper, and finally the woven butterfly.

PAINTED PAPER

This frame-worthy design (right) is a watercolor painting cut first into three parts, then into strips, and woven together with a solid-color paper for a delightful triptych.

PAPYRUS AND SKEWERS

While not technically paper, papyrus has an earthy appeal that needs no further embellishment. (Papyrus is made by layering plant material across each other at right angles to produce a sheet.) Woven with spaces between the "warp" and "weft" strips, it is glued to two bamboo skewers that lift it above the surface of the card.

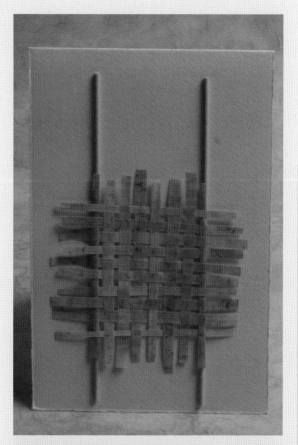

GARDEN PARTY

Think of making party invitations the starting point for a party theme. These two designs, both woven from wallpaper samples, are reminiscent of all things British—a great theme for an afternoon garden party with minted lemonade and cucumber sandwiches.

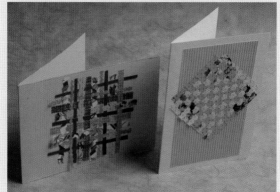

FURTHER READING

If you find you've been bitten by the paper bug, try these resources for some really excellent information.

Silvie Turner's *The Book of Fine Paper* (Thames and Hudson, 1998) is a large-format book produced on lovely paper and full of information about the history of paper and how it's made, as well as kinds of papers and their uses. An excellent reference section informs about sizes and weights, common terminology, and an index of papers.

In Jules Heller's *Paper-Making* (Watson-Guptill Publications, 1978) you'll encounter easily accessible information geared toward the novice. Good instruction is provided for making your own paper including troubleshooting notes. The gallery of work is interesting, and I found the timeline of paper's development fascinating.

An inspiring volume is *The Complete Book of Papermaking* by Josep Asuncion (Lark Books, 2001). Plentiful color photography illustrates lively page layouts that make this book fun to browse. I particularly like the sections on the characteristics of paper, fiber information, and step-by-step projects.

When I was growing up, mealtime was special. My mother insisted on cloth napkins and a tablecloth, and not once did I eat a meal at her table without a bouquet of fresh flowers. Our home was comfortable and familiar, graced by distinctive gifts from family and friends, souvenirs from world travels, and unique, original art. These objects enhanced our surroundings visually. They also connected us to memories and events and the people of our lives. Intentional or not, every day was a celebration of the small things that work in a big way to make life worth living.

Today I try to capture the spirit of my childhood by creating a home that is comfortable and distinctive. Making things is part of creating a place that feels real and memorable. I find a pleasure in my creations that brings both balance and enjoyment to living.

". . . as we go about the creation of who we will be, one price we sometimes pay is that we forget to live. In a culture that richly rewards achievement and accomplishment, it is left to us to create a balanced life, to master the art of creating a life worth living."
—*Wally Arnold from* Illuminations: Living by Candlelight

OVERVIEW: For this pleasingly simple lantern lamp, *woven paper is rolled* into a tube and lit with a tubular bulb. A simple commercially made paper with *flecks of flower petals* is used here, but any paper that allows light to shine through, including handmade papers, will work. *Flexible copper adhesive tape* trims the top and bottom. The light base is made with parts purchased at the *hardware store.*

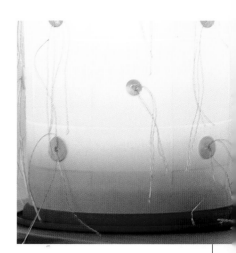

INSTRUCTIONS

MATERIALS AND EQUIPMENT

For shade: One sheet of Strathmore Petal Violet Art Paper, measuring 19 x 25" (48.5 x 63.5 cm); 5/32" (3 mm) wide heat-resistant acrylic adhesive on ductile copper foil, 36" (91.5 cm) long; five 1/16" (2 mm) diameter copper paper fasteners.

For lamp: Porcelain keyless lamp holder with supplied screws; ceiling pan; light cord with on/off switch; 25-watt white tubular light; electrical tape; 6" (15 cm) diameter plastic plant saucer; 6" (15 cm) square of rubber mat; 2 roundhead 3/4" (2 cm) long bolts with nuts and washers (the bolt length may vary depending on the depth of the plastic plant saucer you use).

You'll also need: Cutting mat; rotary cutter; ruler; straight edge; scissors; 3/32" (24 mm) diameter paper punch; hammer; glue stick; pencil; pliers; screwdriver; butterfly clips; drill with 1/4" (6 mm) drill bit; block of scrap wood for use when drilling; pliers; permanent marker.

RESOURCES

Materials for the shade are available at specialty paper, art, and craft stores. Light parts can be found at hardware or lighting stores.

FINISHED SIZE

About 11¾ (30 cm) tall and 5" (12.5 cm) in diameter.

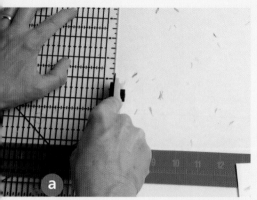

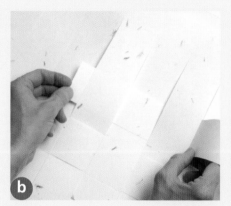

LANTERN

1 Cut 1" (2.5 cm) off the width to make the paper 18" (45.5 cm) wide. (This will be a lengthwise strip.) Then cut 5 wefts, each measuring 2 x 18" (5 x 45.5 cm). Cut the remaining piece so that it measures 13½ x 18" (34.5 x 45.5 cm). Measure and mark lines very lightly with a pencil 1½" (3.8 cm) from each short edge. Measure and mark eight cutting lines 2" (5 cm) apart along the long dimension from pencil line to pencil line. Use an Exacto knife to carefully cut along the 8 marked lines (see figure a). Note: Cut up to, but not through, pencil lines. Before proceeding, roll up the lantern to make sure the sides line up exactly. If not, trim for an exact fit (otherwise the bottom or top of your lantern will be uneven).

2 Weave all 5 wefts in an over-under pattern in the slits cut in the larger piece (see figure b), snugging them up after they are all woven. To prevent the strips from unweaving, secure the ends at the edges with small dots of glue (see figure c).

3 Fold the top and bottom edges over to meet the weaving (fold to your pencil line) and secure with glue stick (see figure d).

4 Apply copper foil tape along the top and bottom edges on the right side of the lantern (see figure e).

5 Punch a hole in the center of each square along one woven edge using a paper punch and hammer (see figure f). To find the center of the square, draw diagonals from corner to corner on the wrong side of the paper; the intersection where the lines cross is the center of the square. Before punching the holes, place the tube around the inverted plant saucer to check that the fit is snug. If it is too loose or too tight, adjust the tube.

6 Make a tube, overlapping the edges so that the first row of squares lines up. Temporarily secure with butterfly clips and use a pencil to mark through the first hole to indicate the placement of its corresponding hole (see figure g). Mark remaining holes in the same way. Punch out these holes using the paper punch and then secure the tube with copper paper fasteners (see figure h).

LAMP

1 Use a hammer and screwdriver to knock out the center hole in the ceiling pan. Place the ceiling pan on the inside of the plant saucer, and using the marker, mark the center and side screw holes, as well as the side of the rim on the inside of the plant saucer to accommodate the electrical cord (see figure a). Place the plant saucer on the wood block and drill the four marked holes with a ¼" (6 mm) drill bit (see figure b).

2 For an added layer of safety, cut the rubber mat to the same circumference as the ceiling pan. Drill a ¼" (6 mm) hole in the center of the mat. Attach the ceiling pan with bolts, nuts, and washers to the top of the inverted plant saucer (see figure c). Fit the rubber mat into the ceiling pan.

3 Thread the electrical cord into the side rim hole and up through the center hole of the plant saucer/ceiling pan unit (see figure d).

4 Loosen the screws in the bottom of the porcelain lamp holder and wrap the wires from the electrical cord around the screws (see figure e). Tighten the screws, using extreme care that the wire ends are secure and not touching each other. Cover the wires with electrical tape. Warning: Be sure to consult with the electrical experts at the hardware store when purchasing the parts for your lamp. It is important to install the wiring carefully so that the wire ends are secure.

5 Screw the lamp holder to the ceiling pan with the supplied screws (see figure f), then screw in the lightbulb. Place the paper lantern over the base, pressing firmly to secure.

LIGHT COLUMN

Opaque Mylar lets light shine through softly. Here, 1" (2.5 cm) and 2" (5 cm) strips are alternated to make woven squares and rectangles. Vintage mother-of-pearl buttons embellish the surface. Light-reflective yarn used to attach the buttons glows when light strikes it, creating a light column that illuminates from within with eerie highlights on the outside.

{*}

HINTS:

+ If you don't have a drill, you can use a mat or utility knife to cut holes in the plant saucer, though the holes will not be as neat as drilled ones.

+ A small lamp with a base that accommodates the paper lantern is a possible substitute for the lamp base shown here.

+ Measure twice, cut once. Because the two sides of the rolled paper tube must match perfectly, it is important to check your measurements as you go to make sure you've measured and cut correctly.

+ Substituting paper: Paper that works best has some weight to it, but is not so thick that light cannot shine through it. Likewise, papers that are too fine to hold their shape but have interesting texture can be used together with a more substantial paper, provided light can still shine through. When deciding if a paper is appropriate, try rolling it up and standing it on end to see if it is sturdy enough. Hold the paper up to light to determine whether it is translucent enough.

OPEN WEAVE

For this variation, I used two different papers, a pale green botanical paper for the vertical elements and an off-white plain paper for the horizontals. I left ¼" (6 mm) spaces between each strip, creating holes for the light to shine through. Copper foil trim stabilizes and protects the edges.

FURTHER READING

These books all have a wealth of information about making lampshades and unique lamps and include clear step-by-step instruction and many inspiring ideas: *The Paper Shade Book* by Maryellen Driscoll (Rockport Publishers, 2001), *The Lamp Shade Book* by Dawn Cusick (Sterling/Lark Books, 1996), and *Making Great Lamps* by Deborah Morgenthal (Lark Books, 1998).

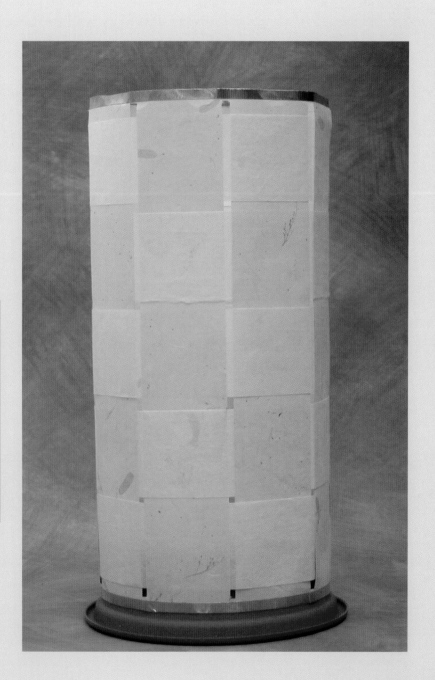

Almost any basket you'll see anywhere has been woven by hand—an amazing fact given our mechanized world. With few exceptions, baskets are three-dimensional woven forms, but the range of techniques and materials used for basketry is vast.

Basketmaking has been practiced since earliest civilizations, and according to textile experts, probably predates pottery. The evidence is found in basket impressions on ancient pottery; the baskets themselves did not survive. Next time you go the natural history or art museum, take some time to seek out the baskets on display. You will be rewarded with wonderment at our textile predecessors' ingenuity and craftsmanship.

Basically, basketry construction is like flat weaving. A base is woven flat with elements called stakes or weavers. These are then bent upward and woven to form the sides. For this basket, the weavers that form the base are woven across each other for the sides in what is referred to as bias plaiting.

"I believe that artists have far greater control of their work when they know about the materials they work with and that through knowledge one becomes better acquainted with the potential of the medium."

—*Silvie Turner*

OVERVIEW: Grocery bags make a plaited basket that is both *attractive and surprisingly sturdy.* Woven in bias plaiting, this woven form is a lot like braiding, with elements woven across each other. If you haven't done this kind of plaiting before, you may feel a little *mystified by how this basket develops.* Just remember, no matter what, *you are always weaving* over-under, over-under.

INSTRUCTIONS

MATERIALS AND EQUIPMENT

Four or five large brown paper grocery bags; string or thread for twining (optional); clothespins; cutting mat; rotary cutter; awl or tapestry needle; scissors; small tweezers.

RESOURCES

Brown paper bags are available at most grocery stores.

FINISHED SIZE

About 6" (15 cm) tall and 7¼" (18.5 cm) in diameter.

HINTS:

+ If using paper that needs to be folded for weaving, cut the strip four times the desired width.

+ Clothespins are invaluable weaving aids. If you are weaving small baskets, alligator clips or tiny clothespins are lightweight alternatives.

+ An even number of elements in both directions is required for this type of basket.

1 To prepare the weavers, carefully cut out the bottom of each bag. With the bag folded, cut 16 rings, each 3½" (8.8 cm) wide, across the width of the bag (see figure a). Cut each ring apart at the seam to get 16 strips that each measure 38" (96.5 cm) long.

2 Fold each strip in half lengthwise, with the printed side facing in to mark the center line. Unfold the strips, fold the outer edges to the center line (see figure b), then fold again along the center line, creasing tightly—the strips will be four layers thick. The more uniform and crisp the weavers, the better your basket will be.

3 Weave a square base in plain weave, using 8 weavers in both directions (see figure c). Point the folds toward the center of each side so the corners will be neater.

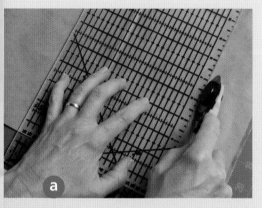

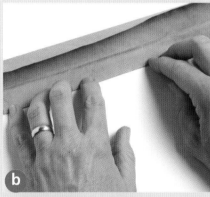

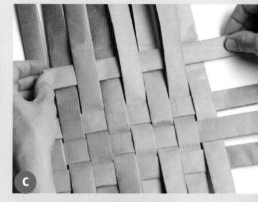

4 Mark the base by twining around the edges with string (see How to Twine, page 23). Once you understand how this basket works, you might find that you can eliminate this step, although I like to twine because it allows me to better see what's going on (see figure d).

5 Working one side at a time, divide the weavers in half (two groups of four) and weave the halves together (see figure e). Beginning with the center weavers, cross them and weave both out to the edge. Weave the second, third, and fourth weavers in the same manner. Tighten the weavers by pulling gently on them. The weaving will poke out where the weavers cross to form the new corner. When all 4 weavers on this side have been woven, you'll have a woven diamond (see figure f). Secure this side with clothespins. Repeat for the other three sides.

6 Join the diamonds by weaving them together until your basket is as tall as you want it to be (see figures g, h). Notice that if you follow one weaver, it travels from one side of the basket to the other. Remove the twining.

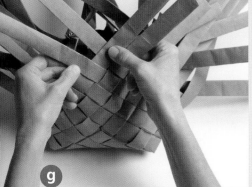

7 To make a nice pointy top, take 2 weavers that cross at the edge and fold one over the other and down into the weaving on the inside (see figure i). Use an awl to open up the space in the weaving if you have trouble sliding the weaver into the weaving. It can also help to grab the end of the weaver with a tweezers to pull it through. Repeat for the other one. Do likewise with all the weavers. If you have holes in the bottom or sides of your basket, it means that it is not tightly woven. You can fix this by pulling the weavers from the bottom of the basket to the top and taking out the extra length by pulling on the weaver on the inside of the basket. Keep tightening weavers until they are snug against each other. You may find this tedious, but it is well worth the effort in the finished basket. Once you're satisfied with the tightness of the weave, check the top edge to see that it's even and then trim the weavers on the inside.

FURTHER READING

Here are some of my favorite basketry books.

In *The Techniques of Basketry* (University of Washington Press, 1986), author Virginia I. Harvey briefly explores the history of basketry and then explores several specific basketry techniques. While her instructions are brief, I find her examples of ethnic, historical, and present day baskets especially inspiring.

If you become very keen on plaiting, the volume you want to get your hands on is the long out-of-print, self-published book, *Plaited Basketry: The Woven Form* by Shereen LaPlantz (Press de LaPlantz, 1982). After studying LaPlantz's plaiting explorations, you'll realize how boundless this technique is. The Internet makes finding this gem a possibility.

Baskets from Nature's Bounty by Elizabeth Jensen (Interweave Press, 1991) is another book that I'd love to see back in print. Provided here are lots of good solid basketry technique how-tos and excellent detailed information about collecting and using natural materials for basketmaking.

Making the New Baskets (Lark Books, 1999) is a hoot. In this handsome, colorful volume, author Jane LaFerla uses materials as diverse as plastic tubing and polypropylene strapping tape.

VARIATIONS

READ ALL ABOUT IT

The Sunday funny papers are a colorful choice for basket weaving. I chose the funnies with the brightest colors (near right). To stiffen and protect the basket, I painted it inside and out with white glue. A monochromatic alternative is the basket at far right, woven from pages where I deliberately avoided colorful photos and looked for small print, such as want ads. After weaving, I treated the surface with melted bees' wax for a muted and aged appearance.

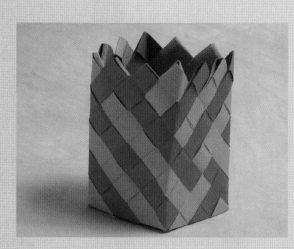

COLOR PLAY

It's fun to see what happens when colors are woven together. For the small basket below, I used ½" (1.3 cm) weavers made from colored craft paper. I alternated red and gold in both directions for striped patterns. Creasing gives this basket straight sides.

GARDEN BASKET

This small basket (left) is woven with iris leaves from my garden. I cut them close to the ground in the fall and laid them flat to dry. Just before weaving, I soaked them in the bathtub with warm water, adding a couple of teaspoons of glycerin to soften them. I rolled them in a towel for a couple of hours to further condition them. To keep the leaves moist during weaving, I sprayed them with water as I worked. The edge is made by simply folding down the weavers and trimming. I shaped the top by folding out the points as the basket dried.

Sometimes it is hard to make design decisions because there is too much to decide. How long? How wide? Should there be stripes? If so, where? How many and how wide? How many colors? Which ones?

Not a panacea, but a helpful design tool, is the Fibonacci series of numbers. Fibonacci (born Leonardo Pisano) was a twelfth-century mathematician who is best remembered today for what is known as the Fibonacci sequence. It works like this: each number in the series is the sum of the two preceding numbers: 1 + 1 = 2, 1 + 2 = 3, 2 +3 = 5, 3 + 5 = 8, and so on. (He came up with this sequence as an exercise in describing a reproductive pattern for rabbits where at first there is a newborn pair.) As it turns out, the ratio of two successive numbers, for example 5 and 8, is also the gold ratio 1:1.61803. It's the same ratio the Greeks used to design the Parthenon in 400 B.C. It translates to a rectangle of which the long side is 1.61803 times as long as the short side.

The golden rectangle is special because it is the only rectangle from which a square can be cut and the remaining rectangle retain the same proportion as the first. This rectangle can be divided again and again with always the same proportional result.

Studying further, the golden ratio is found throughout nature, in the number of petals on many flowers, or the spirals found in seashells. Using the Fibonacci sequence and the golden ratio are helpful in designing because these ratios are part of the world we live in. They are innately familiar to us. Use the Fibonacci for helping decide the width and length of a piece, the number of colors, the placement of stripes and design elements. These are handy tools to use when all the little decisions are holding you back.

OVERVIEW: This window hanging, *designed with the aid of the Fibonacci series,* softens a view but still lets the light in. The base (warp) is heavy plastic sheeting cut into strips through which *organdy ribbon* (weft) has been woven. Because the plastic is fairly rigid, it allows the soft, floppy ribbon to *waft in and out* of it. I allowed extra ribbon and *pulled out the loops* to exaggerate the effect.

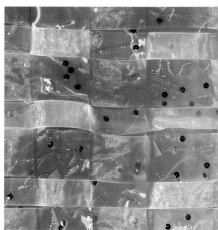

INSTRUCTIONS

MATERIALS AND EQUIPMENT

14 x 34" (35.5 x 86.5 cm) piece of 5 mm plastic sheeting; 1½" (3.8 cm) wide organdy ribbon, 85" (2.12 m) white, 51" (129.5 cm) each of yellow and gold; ½" (1.3 cm) wide organdy ribbon, 68" (1.7 m) white, 51" (129.5 cm) each of yellow and gold; two ½" (1.3 cm) diameter acrylic rods, each 16" (40.5 cm) long; cutting mat; mat knife; rotary cutter; quilting rule; scissors; masking tape; 3M Safe Release Painter's Masking Tape; sewing machine and thread; tweezers; fish line for hanging.

"And the day came when the risk to remain in a tight bud was more painful than the risk it took to blossom."

—Anais Nin

RESOURCES

The plastic sheeting and acrylic rods are available at hardware stores; ribbons can be found at fabric, quilting, and craft stores.

FINISHED SIZE

About 16 x 28" (40.5 x 71 cm).

HINTS:

+ Doing all the work on the grid of the cutting mat makes this project easy.

+ Set your machine for short stitches. This perforates the plastic more and simplifies removing the tape.

+ Measure twice, cut once.

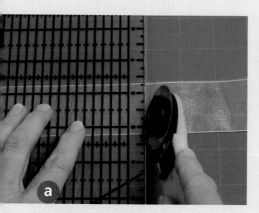

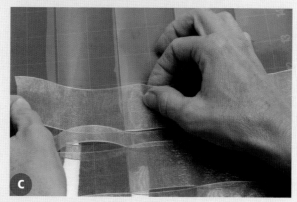

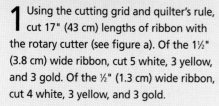

1 Using the cutting grid and quilter's rule, cut 17" (43 cm) lengths of ribbon with the rotary cutter (see figure a). Of the 1½" (3.8 cm) wide ribbon, cut 5 white, 3 yellow, and 3 gold. Of the ½" (1.3 cm) wide ribbon, cut 4 white, 3 yellow, and 3 gold.

2 Cut a piece of plastic 14 x 34" (35.5 x 86.5 cm). Using the grid on the cutting mat, measure 6" (15 cm) down from the top and 6" (15 cm) up from the bottom (short sides). Place a piece of masking tape across the entire width of the plastic at the 6" marks. Secure the plastic on the cutting mat with a couple of pieces of masking tape, lining up the plastic with the grid. Using mat knife and quilter's rule, cut 2" (5 cm) wide strips, each 22" (56 cm) long, beginning at the strip of masking tape at the top and ending at the strip of masking tape at the bottom (see figure b). Do not cut through the tape. These plastic strips are your warps.

3 Weave over-under, over-under, alternating 1½" (3.8 cm) and ½" (1.3 cm) ribbon, beginning and ending with 1½" (3.8 cm) ribbon (see figure c). Use the color order shown at right.

1" RIBBON	½" RIBBON
YELLOW	
	WHITE
WHITE	
	GOLD
WHITE	
	YELLOW
GOLD	
	WHITE
GOLD	
	YELLOW
YELLOW	
	GOLD
WHITE	
	WHITE
YELLOW	
	WHITE
GOLD	
	YELLOW
WHITE	
	GOLD
WHITE	

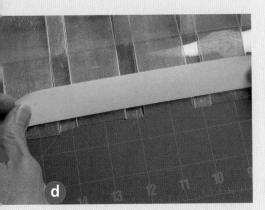

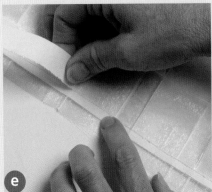

4 Adjust the ribbons at the edges, making sure they are evenly spaced and not overlapping. Ribbon should hang out ½" (1.3 cm) at the edge. Take care with this step, as it ensures that your weaving will be tidy. Work one edge at a time. When everything is lined up, use the safe release masking tape to secure the ribbon along the edge of the outside warp on the front and the back (see figure d). Repeat for the other side.

5 Machine stitch as closely as possible to the edge using the tape as a guide. Repeat for other side. Tear off tape as you would rip off paper from a tablet (see figure e). Use tweezers to clean off any bits of tape left in the stitching. Fold over hems to where the weaving starts, making 3" (7.5 cm) hems at top and bottom. Because the plastic makes it difficult to see where to stitch, use tape as a stitching guide. Trim ribbon along edges to ⅜" (1 cm) and trim threads.

6 Insert acrylic rods in top and bottom hems. Tie fishing line on either side of the top rod using square knots (see figure f). If the fishing line slides over when you hang the hanging, place a small dot of epoxy glue on the rod at the inside edge of the knot.

FURTHER READING

I love traditional textiles as much as those using nontraditional materials and techniques. Currently a great deal of experimentation is going on with yarn, finishing techniques, construction, and finishing methods. A few books to check out are the Nuno Books, a series of fabric picture books with brief explanations. This series, published by Nuno Corporation, a Japanese company, features different fabric ideas with large, appealing pictures. *Techno Textiles* (Thames and Hudson, 2001) is a collection of essays about different aspects of current fabric development and includes excellent photographs of some amazing and sometimes outrageous fabrics. Another English publisher, Telos, is publishing monograph-style books on art weaving, profiling individual artists and their work, as well as art textiles by country. If you're wondering about art weaving, these are the places to look.

VARIATIONS

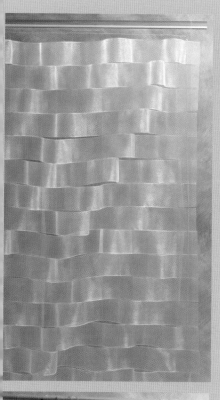

WHITE WAVES

A twill weave—an over-two, under-two stepped sequence—was used for this ephemeral hanging (left). Generous lengths of weft are pulled into exaggerated waves that undulate across the width.

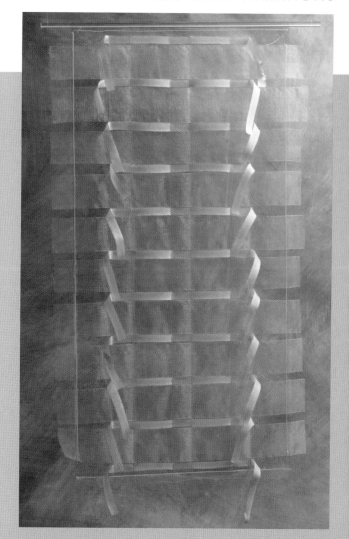

ALL THAT GLITZ

Bits and pieces of fabric and yarn and leftover sequins are encased between a sheet of clear Contac Paper and lightweight clear plastic sheeting (left). This plastic sandwich was then cut in 2" (5 cm) strips and woven with alternating 1½" (3.8 cm) and ½" (1.3 cm) organdy ribbon.

PASTEL ESCAPE

Silk organdy ribbon alternated with a space-dyed silk bias-cut ribbon are interwoven in a warp of alternating thick and thin strips (above). The wider organdy ribbons are stitched along the edge, but the bias silk ribbons are allowed to hang, free to move gently in the breeze.

I f we think we know more than our forebears, we only need to look at the ancient textiles they produced. How did they know to coax useable fiber out of a plant stalk and twist it to make strong rope? How did they weave a basket so tight it could hold water for weeks at a time? And how in the world did they figure out that the little bugs living on a prickly cactus made a permanent, vibrant red dye? These ancients should not only be venerated for their resourcefulness, they should be admired for accomplishing so much with little else than their own two hands. It was with those clever but primitive ancestors in mind that I went searching for the solution to the design problem for these coasters.

I wanted a coaster that would sit still on the table—a hefty, sturdy, yet open structure. I tried twining, a common basket technique, but found it did not easily produce the open, rigid result I sought. After searching through a lot of books, I found what I was looking for in Peter Collingwood's *The Makers Hand* (Interweave Press, 1987) and again in Hideyuki Oka's *How to Wrap Five Eggs* (Harper and Row, 1967). Here I found an ancient structure, simple but elegant, used by peoples in completely different parts of the world. It's a simple two-loop technique—no fancy equipment is necessary.

OVERVIEW: Two long loops of string (the warp) are *passed through each other* to hold slats (the weft) in place. Working one row at a time, insert a slat, bring the top loop *through the bottom loop,* and repeat. Each two-loop warp row is worked until all of the slats have been inserted. The other two-loop warp *rows are worked* in the same way. This structure is *surprisingly sturdy*—excellent for any item that needs to be strong but open, such as a placemat or *window shade.*

INSTRUCTIONS

MATERIALS AND EQUIPMENT

Micro-cut scale basswood strips, about ¼ x 11"
(6 x 28 cm); #72 cotton cable cord, just under
5 yd (45 m); a 2" (5 cm) length of ½" (1.3 cm)
diameter electrical shrink tubing, cut into eight
¼" (6 mm) sections (you can substitute small
black rubber bands, but they will not last as long
as the shrink tubing; alternatively, you can bind
the loop cord with black yarn or thread); scissors
or garden shears; masking tape; ruler; pencil; hair
dryer.

RESOURCES

Hardware and hobby stores stock cable cord and
basswood strips (these typically come in 10-piece
bags at craft and hobby stores; one bag will
make two coasters); electrical shrink tubing is
available at hardware stores. (The rubber bands
can be purchased at the grocery store in the hair-
care section, if you decide to use them instead of
shrink tubing.)

FINISHED SIZE

About 5½ x 6¼" (14 x 16 cm).

*"Ethnic crafts provide a
wellspring of inspiration for design,
technique, shape,
and form."*

—Jane Patrick

{*}

HINTS:

+ *It is easiest to begin the first row of loops in the center
  of the slats and then work out towards the sides.*

+ *Cable cord frays readily, so secure it right away.*

+ *After each row, snug up the cords by pulling up on the
  loops to take out any leftover slack.*

1 For each coaster, cut ten 5½" (14 cm) lengths of basswood strips using garden shears. Cut 8 cords, each 20" (51 cm) long. Cut eight ¼" (6 mm) lengths of shrink tubing.

2 Fold 2 cords in half and secure the cut ends with shrink tubing 1½" (3.8 cm) from the end. Repeat with remaining cords, for a total of four pairs of cords. Use a hair dryer set on high to shrink the tubing around the cords (see figure a), and then adjust the cords so that the loops are the same length.

3 Tape a pair of cords to your work surface. To weave the first row, lift up one loop and insert a strip between the two loops (see figure b). Next, pass the top loop through the bottom loop (see figure c).

a

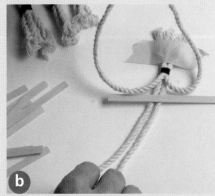

b

c

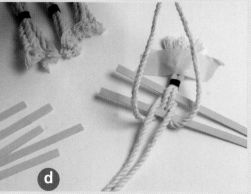

d

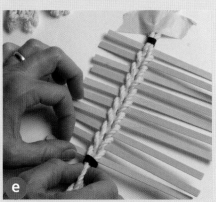

e

f

4 To weave the second row, pass the top loop through the bottom loop, then insert another strip between the two loops (see figure d). Repeat until all 10 strips have been inserted.

5 Tighten the loops by pulling on them and pushing the strips together so that they are held firmly by the loops. Secure with shrink tubing (see figure e).

6 Repeat for the other three looped pairs (see figure f). Shrink the tubing with the hair dryer. Finish by cutting the end loops, unraveling the cord to make a fringe, and trim to ¾" (2 cm).

VARIATIONS

FLOWER STALKS AND RAFFIA MAT

Sometimes you need only look as far as your own back yard to find weaving materials. For this rustic mat (right), I cut flower stems in late fall, dried them thoroughly, and then wove them with natural raffia. Tree branch trimmings would also make appealing strips, especially if the bark had interesting texture and color.

BAMBOO AND SHELL TABLE MAT

Bamboo is readily available and excellent for many practical household objects. For the mat below, I cut bamboo garden stakes with pruning loppers, sanding rough ends as necessary. I wove them together with natural cotton cable string and finished the ends with shells I've gathered over the years from various trips to the seashore. The mat is functional and practical, but it also captures memories of sunny, salty, carefree days. A few beads, leftovers from other projects, add a hint of color.

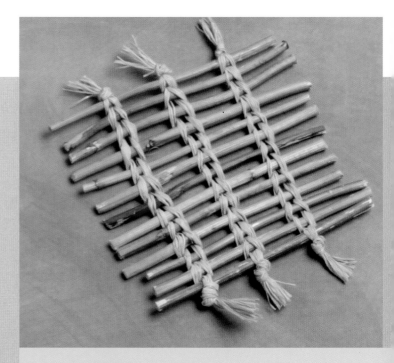

FURTHER READING

Here are three books I turn to again and again for inspiration from traditional textiles and techniques. They are informative and beautifully presented. *How to Wrap Five Eggs* by Hideyuki Oka (Harper and Row, 1967) is an oversized volume with large black-and-white photos. This book showcases traditional Japanese methods of packaging, many of which employ textile techniques. Everyday objects are presented as works to be admired. They never fail to inspire me. The back of the book includes short narratives about each piece and highlights its use, history, and method of construction.

Another book devoted to Japanese craft is Hisako Sekijima's *Basketry Projects from Baskets to Grass Slippers* (Kodansha International, 1986). This how-to book shows in simple detailed line drawings how to make any number of useful objects.

One of my favorite books for studying the ingeniousness of indigenous textiles is Peter Collingwood's *A Maker's Hand* (Interweave Press, 1987). The objects collected in this volume are beautifully photographed by David Cripps and are accompanied by historical information and line drawings. The objects therein are a testament to human ingenuity for blending practical function with timeless beauty. This is a most fascinating and useful resource.

So now I've told you about my favorite books. Too bad they're all out-of-print. However, today, thanks to the Internet, these treasures are often easy to locate just searching by title and author. All three are well worth the search.

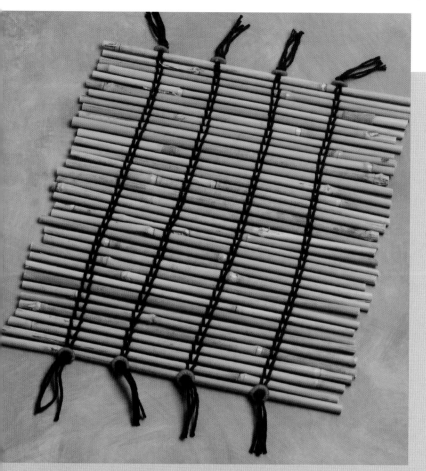

BAMBOO WITH RED AND BLACK

Choosing materials and colors can evoke a time or place or culture. To suggest the Orient, I've used red and black accents with natural bamboo for a mat with clean, understated lines (left). The red disks are ordinary metal washers wrapped with red, 3/2 pearl cotton. Embroidery floss would work as well. They are secured with simple overhand knots.

BRASS NUTS AND DOWEL MAT

The hardware store is a great resource for interesting materials. For the long, narrow mat at the left, I've worked flat black braid over sanded and oiled ¼" (6 mm) dowels. Sometimes, very small details can make a big difference—like these brass nuts and multicolored rubber bands that turn the serious to playful.

TILE WRAP

Here's a simple idea: wrap a tile with yarn, thread, or string in one direction to form a warp and then weave across in the other. A set of three tiles makes an attractive wall accent and is an excellent way to recycle leftover tiles.

Weaving can be more than over-under, over-under, as these tile wraps illustrate. Infinite interlacement variations are possible by simply changing the number of warps the weft travels over or under.

I've woven over and under three warps at a time for these tile wraps. For the first tile, I wove over three and under three 3 times and then switched the order for the next three rows. For the other two tiles, I again used units of three but varied the interlacement. Before weaving, I first worked out the designs on graph paper with no more than 15 warps or wefts in either direction.

> "Anyone can make the simple complicated.
> Creativity is making the complicated simple."
>
> —Charles Mingus

OVERVIEW:

Contrasts of *soft and hard* work together to make these easy-as-pie decorative wall tiles. All you have to do is *wrap the tile* in one direction and then *weave across it* in the other. For a rustic look, I used 6" (15 cm) square tumbled quartzite tiles in sage and *a natural white paper yarn.* I wove each tile with a different interlacement, always using units of three for *design unity.*

INSTRUCTIONS

MATERIALS AND EQUIPMENT

Three 6" (15 cm) square quartzite tiles in sage; twisted paper yarn in off-white, 33 yd (30 m) of yarn will make all three tiles; masking tape; white glue such as Elmers; 5-minute epoxy; three ⅝" (1.5 cm) brass picture hangers; six ½" (1.3 cm) clear vinyl bumpers; tapestry needle; scissors; ruler; craft sticks or toothpicks to apply glue and press down on object being glued; ruler; pencil.

RESOURCES

Quartzite tiles are available from tile and stone vendors. (I used tiles leftover from a household project.) The paper yarn is from Habu Textiles. You can also substitute paper wrapping material or cotton butcher string.

FINISHED SIZE

Each tile measures 6 x 6" (15 x 15 cm).

Diagrams for Tile Wrap Variations

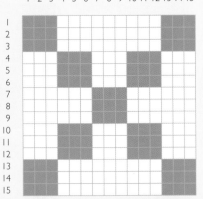

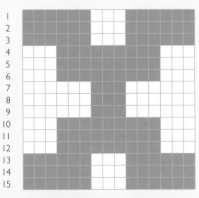

Each row represents one weft yarn; each column represents one warp yarn.
Shaded boxes indicate weft yarns on top of warp yarns.

{*}

HINTS:

+ To keep the back of the tile as flat as possible, be sure that yarns do not cross over each other as you wind.

+ Tighten as you go, pulling up on each round to take up any slack.

1 Choose the best side of the tile for the front. On the back side, mark a line 2" (5 cm) in from each corner on all four sides. Cut 5 yd (4.5 m) of paper yarn and secure the beginning with a dab of glue at one of the points where the marked lines cross (see figure a). Let dry until fully set.

2 Wind yarn around the tile 15 times (see figure b). Adjust the wrapping so that it is snug and evenly spaced within the two guidelines. Be sure that the wrapping does not cross itself. Cut the yarn and temporarily secure the end to the tile with masking tape.

3 Measure about 5½ yd (5 m) of paper yarn for the weft. To begin weaving, secure the end with glue on the back 2" (5 cm) from the edge. Thread the yarn on a tapestry needle and weave the first row over 3, under 3 all the way across (see figure c). Take the yarn around the back, return to the front, and weave the same path as before, repeating for a total of three wefts in the same path. Weave the next three rows under 3, over 3. Repeat these two steps until a total of 15 rows are woven. Temporarily secure the yarn end with masking tape.

a

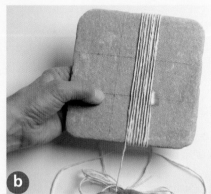

b

c

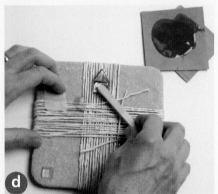

d

4 Beginning at the center of the weaving, press the wefts tightly together on all four sides, repeating for all the rows until the weaving is very tight with no spaces in between. Even out the wraps along the edges as needed so that they are evenly spaced.

5 Press a rubber bumper on both bottom corners on the back of the tile. Find the center of the top edge of the tile, measure down 1" (2.5 cm). Place a generous amount of 5-minute epoxy over the yarn at this point and then place the hook on top, pressing down firmly with the craft stick

until fully set (see figure d). Secure the yarn ends with glue. Follow the diagrams on the facing page for weaving the other two tile wraps in the same manner.

VARIATIONS

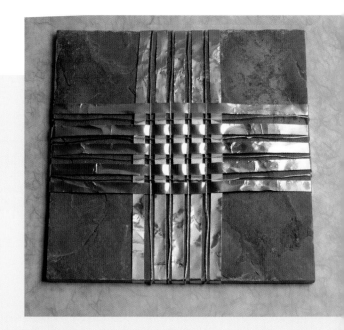

COPPER AND STONE

A study in contrast, this 12" (30.5 cm) square of dull green granite is wrapped with shiny ½" (1.3 cm) copper foil and copper wire. Alternating foil and wire creates an interesting dimensional weave. The structure is my favorite plain weave—over, under, over, under—but it looks different because two different materials are used.

RAFFIA WRAP

The ever-so-slight variation in this natural raffia makes an interesting weave offset by pale green tumbled quartzite.

FURTHER READING

You may find that after doing a few tile wraps that you are intrigued with what happens with colors in a woven fabric. The relativity of color is what I find fascinating. You just never know what will happen to one color until you place it next to another. Below are a few of my favorite resources.

For an in-depth, scholarly look at color, Johannes Itten's *The Elements of Color* (Van Nostrand Reinhold, 1970) is comprehensive and includes excellent color plates. A volume written just for fiber crafters is Deb Menz's *Color Works* (Interweave Press, 2004). The color novice will appreciate the approachability of her writing, the organization of the material, and the excellent color illustration. Included in the book are perforated hue cards, gray scale, and color wheel—great for gaining deeper understanding of color. Two other books I go to when I'm trying to decide on a color theme are the series of ``Designer's Guide to Color" books (Chronicle Books) that present literally thousands of color combinations. I like perusing these when I'm stuck and usually find an idea or combination I hadn't thought of previously.

CATTY-WOMPUS TILE

A novelty cotton and paper yarn is woven in an over-under pattern for this tile, with slanting yarns and random spacing reminiscent of rock fractures. This is a wonderful way to showcase a novelty or handspun yarn, or natural materials from your garden.

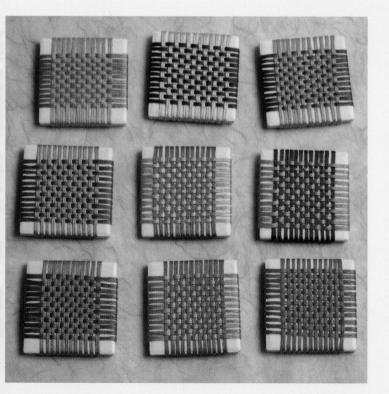

PETITE TILE WRAPS

Two-inch tiles are the perfect size for experimenting with color. For these mini weavings, I used embroidery floss to explore a variety of color combinations. For one set, I explored color by crossing one color with another. Colors similar in value create a harmonious effect. For the other set, the tile forms the background for color plaid designs. Attaching a clasp or a magnet to the back transforms these color studies into functional objects. Designed by Jessica Knickman.

Braiding is related to weaving in that threads weave over and under each other. However in braiding, the threads intersect obliquely instead of at right angles as in a woven structure. Braiding and weaving also differ in that in weaving warp and weft are two distinct sets of threads—the warp (vertical threads) and the weft (horizontal threads). In braiding, all the threads serve both purposes. Warp threads cross each other as wefts, then become warps again. I've included braiding in this book because of the basic over-under interlacement it shares with weaving.

Because braiding requires little more than something to anchor the threads to and your own hands, it is easy to understand why it was developed in ancient times. We know people have been making braids as long ago as 8000 B.C. from evidence discovered in pottery remains. Similar braids have been found in cultures throughout the world made by people who most likely never contacted each other, yet found similar solutions to the same problems. Throughout their long history, braids have performed countless practical as well as ceremonial purposes.

"The heart has reasons that the mind knows nothing of . . ."
—*Blaise Pascal*

OVERVIEW: Threads and beads combine to *make this elegant necklace* fit for an evening out on the town. Muted colors in dusty shades of *mauve, green, brown, and gray* create a subtle pointillist effect that plays off the beaded tassel. Use the same technique in *clear, bright Caribbean hues,* and you're ready for a night of reggae.

INSTRUCTIONS

MATERIALS AND EQUIPMENT

48" (122 cm) lengths of embroidery floss in 7 colors (DMC brand color numbers)—dusty rose #3041, golden brown #3787, lavender-gray #414, blue-gray #413, dark gray #844, steely gray #3799, and taupe #3790; nine (6 decorative and 3 plain) silver beads with a ¼" (6 mm) diameter hole; size 11° seed beads in dusty pink and gray; 6 mm faceted glass beads, 20 each in gray and pink; size 10° silver-lined round beads, 40 pink; weight, clip, or tape to anchor braid; scissors; fabric glue; #10 beading needle; small tapestry needle.

RESOURCES

Look for beads in craft and specialty shops; embroidery floss is available at sewing, yarn, and craft stores.

FINISHED SIZE

Braid is ¼" (6 mm) wide; necklace is 16" (40.5 cm) long, including tassel.

HINTS:

+ Keep an even tension while working the braid to ensure even edges.

+ If you need to stop in the middle of making a braid, tie the two working groups into loose knots. When you're ready to work again, untie the knots and the ends will be ready to work from where you left off.

+ Use a needle threader to help in threading the tiny eye in the beading needle.

1 Measure two 48" (122 cm) lengths of every color except dark gray #844 and steely gray #3799; measure 4 lengths of each of these. Gather up all ends and secure them with an overhand knot, leaving a 7" (18 cm) tail for making the beaded tassel

later. Use same-color pairs as if they were one strand, for a total of 9 working strands (see figure a). Separate the steely gray and dark gray pairs so that they are not next to each other.

2 Follow the instructions for How to Make a 9-Strand Braid on page 68 until braid measures 28" (71 cm), being careful to keep the edges smooth and even (see figure b).

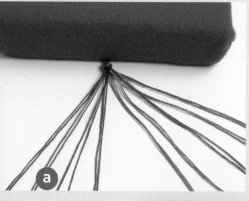

a

b

c

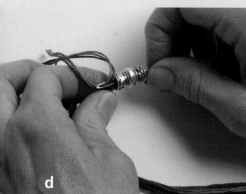

d

e

3 Thread the silver beads onto the braid in sets of three in this order: decorative, plain, decorative. Fold the braid in half and thread the other end of the braid through the last set of beads (see figure c). All of the floss tails should hang out of the last set of 3 beads. If you have trouble sliding all of the strands through the 3 beads, thread a few of them at a time on a tapestry needle and use the needle to guide them through the beads (see figure d).

4 For the tassel, you'll want an equal number of pink and gray bead strings. Thread 2 strands of floss through the #10 beading needle, then for the gray strands, string 40–45 gray beads to equal 2½" (6.5 cm), and then add 1 gray faceted bead, 1 pink silver-lined bead, and 1 pink seed bead. For the pink strands, thread 40–45 pink seed beads, 1 pink faceted bead, 1 pink silver-lined bead, and 1 pink seed bead.

5 The last seed bead holds the string of beads together. Go around the outside of it and then back up through the entire string of beads (see figure e). Pull to tighten and clip off the floss. Repeat until 20 each of gray and pink bead strings have been strung, choosing different ends from different floss strands for the tassel. You will not use all of the floss strands for the beads.

6 To secure the unbeaded floss ends, slide the 3 silver beads up and out of the way, cut off any remaining floss strands (see figure f). Carefully secure the ends with fabric glue (see figure g). Let dry, then slide the beads down to cover the floss ends and adjust the two sets of silver beads on either side of the necklace.

TECHNIQUES

HOW TO MAKE A 9-STRAND BRAID

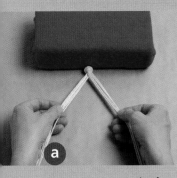

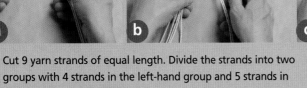

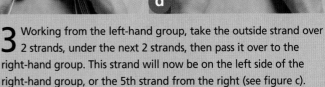

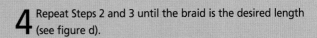

1 Cut 9 yarn strands of equal length. Divide the strands into two groups with 4 strands in the left-hand group and 5 strands in the right-hand group (see figure a).

2 Beginning with the right-hand group, take the outside strand over 2 strands, under the next 2 strands, then pass it over to the left-hand group (this strand will now be on the right side of the left-hand group, or the 5th strand from the left). The left-hand group now has 5 strands (see figure b).

3 Working from the left-hand group, take the outside strand over 2 strands, under the next 2 strands, then pass it over to the right-hand group. This strand will now be on the left side of the right-hand group, or the 5th strand from the right (see figure c).

4 Repeat Steps 2 and 3 until the braid is the desired length (see figure d).

VARIATIONS

BEADED CHOKERS

Beads are added to the edges as the braid is worked (right). The beads are threaded on a strand at the beginning and then slid into place when that thread appears along the edge. A vintage clay pendant adds a bit of hippy funk to the lower choker. Designed by Jessica Knickman.

BLANKET OR SCARF TRIM

A plain fabric is trimmed with this unusual braid, illustrating that you don't need to use the same kind of yarn. Wool in wine and two shades of gray is mixed with unbleached linen and 5/2 aqua pearl cotton. The variation in texture, color, and size creates an undulating result in the braid. Designed by Jessica Knickman.

FURTHER READING

To explore beading further, check out these excellent resources. *The Beader's Companion* by Judith Durant and Jean Campbell (Interweave Press, 1998) is a spiral-bound take-along reference encompassing all the beading basics, including types of beads, thread and cord, needles, stitches, stringing, and more. Another excellent resource is Sharon Bateman's *Findings and Finishings* (Interweave Press, 2003) with detailed information about materials and tools, clasps, connectors, finish knotting, and anchoring.

To learn more about beads themselves, *The Book of Beads* by Janet Coles and Robert Budwig (Simon and Schuster, 1990) is a picture book of sorts that provides a catalog of kinds of beads and presents information about design guidelines, techniques, and ideas for making beautiful beaded objects.

Peter Owens's *The Book of Decorative Knots* (Lyons and Burford, 1994) has super straightforward drawings for all kinds of knots and braids. Very little text is contained in this volume; it is really a compendium of knots but includes a few braids. If you get into braiding in a big way, get your hands on a copy of *Making Kumihimo: Japanese Interlaced Braids* by Rodrick Owen (Guild of Master Craftsmen Publications Ltd, 2004). Here you'll find excellent instruction, plentiful patterns, and many ideas for making exquisite braids.

The following out-of-print book is worth searching the Web for. Don't be put off by the modest appearance of *Finishes in the Ethnic Tradition* by Suzanne Baizerman and Karen Searle (Dos Tejedoras, 1978). This slim volume with superior line drawings is a great reference manual for edge finishes, joins, and embellishments, including braids.

SPRING AND STRING CHOKER

Braiding, like knitting, is handwork that can be taken along almost anywhere. As a Girl Scout leader at day camp, I carried embroidery floss in my backpack, always at the ready for braiding when a diversion was needed. Without exception, the girls found quiet in braiding. Braiding allowed them to relax and chat with one another—and I wasn't nagging them to "calm down."

One day I was surprised and pleased when my daughter, Nora, who was about ten at the time, started braiding as we waited for an appointment. She had cut long lengths of embroidery floss, wrapped them around her ankle, and stored them under the cuff of her sock. When she wanted to braid, she simply unwrapped the floss and anchored it to her sneaker with a safety pin. I don't know how long she'd been doing this, but I was delighted both with her ingenuity and that the seed I had unknowingly sown had taken root.

"Craft, like art, comes from the hand and the doing and re-doing,
from seeing, hearing and thinking, over and over again."
—Octavio Paz and the World Craft Council
In Praise of Hands: Contemporary Crafts of the World

OVERVIEW: Even *simple string* can make a handsome accessory, as this choker illustrates. The structure of the *eight-strand round braid* is shown to excellent advantage by using a hard-twist cotton cable cord—appealing in its *unadorned simplicity.* Because the cord is bulky, traditional jewelry closures were too small. In searching for a solution, I spied a *spring display* at the hardware store—and the solution to my problem.

INSTRUCTIONS

MATERIALS AND EQUIPMENT

#24 cotton cable cord, 5½ yd (5 m); two
7 mm jump (split) rings; one extension spring
measuring ⁷⁄₁₆ x 1¹⁵⁄₁₆" (1.4 x 3 cm), cut in half;
toggle clasp; 5-minute epoxy; toothpicks;
scissors; masking tape; weight or heavy safety
pin; pliers; wire cutter; matching sewing thread;
safety glasses.

RESOURCES

Hardware stores supply all the parts you'll need
for this project.

FINISHED SIZE

About ⅜ x 13" (1 x 33 cm), without fastener.

HINTS:

+ Tighten the braid as you work by pulling back on the
  strands after each pass.

+ If you need to leave your work before it is finished, lay the
  braid down with the yarns in place so that you can pick it
  up where you left off (it is easy to lose your place when
  working this braid).

+ If you make an error, the best way to find your place again
  is to start in the center where two yarns cross. Hold these
  yarns in place and then work back side to side to line up
  four strands on either side of the middle. Check to see
  that the strands are stepped up the sides, one following
  the next, and begin again.

1 Measure 8 strands of cord, each 24" (61 cm) long. Tie an overhand knot and work braid for about 15" (38 cm), following How to Make an 8-Strand Braid instructions on page 74 (see figure a). Because this cord ravels easily, I tied knots in all of the ends. Check cord length around your neck to see if it is the correct length and adjust as needed. Keep in mind that the closure plus spring rings will add about 2" (5 cm) to the overall length.

2 Wrap the ends tightly with sewing thread (see figure b) to prevent raveling. Trim the ends.

3 With wire cutters, cut the spring in half (see figure c). Safety caution: Because the pieces may fly apart when you cut the spring, wear protective glasses to protect your eyes, and hold the spring away from your body and any persons or animals nearby. The smaller gauge the spring wire, the easier it will be to cut.

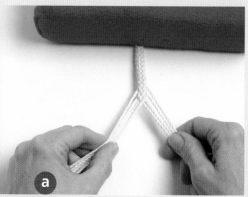

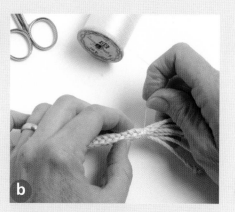

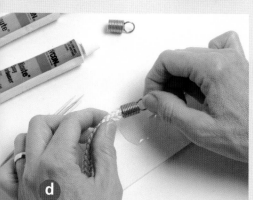

4 Prepare epoxy and then using a toothpick, apply to the inside of the spring. Working one end of the braid at a time, spread epoxy on the end of the braid and then slide it into the spring (see figure d). Immediately clean off any excess epoxy with another toothpick. Allow epoxy to set before gluing the other end.

5 Attach the springs to the toggle closure with jump rings (see figure e).

TECHNIQUES

HOW TO MAKE AN 8-STRAND BRAID

1 Cut 8 strands of equal length. Tie the ends together with an overhand knot and secure to a table. Weight or anchor the braid so that it is held securely (see figure a). Divide the 8 strands into two groups, 4 in your right hand and 4 in your left.

2 Pass the outermost right-hand strand under 5 strands (3 in the right-hand group and 2 in the left-hand group; see figure b) and back over 2 strands (the same 2 in the left-hand group you just went under), then return this strand to the right-hand group. It is now on the left-hand edge of the right-hand group, or the 4th strand from the right (see figure c).

3 Now do exactly the same working from the left. Take the outermost left-hand strand under 5 strands (3 in the left-hand group and 2 in the right-hand group), back over 2 (the same 2 you just went under), then return this strand to the left side. It will now be the 4th strand from the left (see figure d).

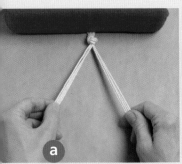
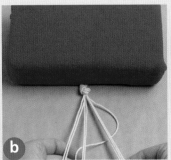

4 Repeat Steps 2 and 3 until the braid is the desired length—it will take several repeats before the pattern emerges (see figure e).

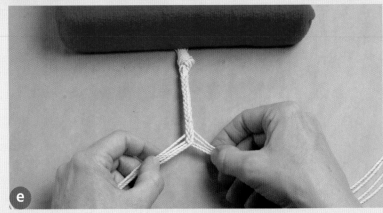

FURTHER READING

See page 69 for notes on braiding resources.

VARIATIONS

PLAY WITH COLOR

These three bands at the right use pairs of colors for patterning. All are made with the same 8-strand braid structure. The only difference is in the number of different colors used. Threading orders are, top to bottom: ABBB, BBBA; AABC, CBAA; ABCD, DCBA.

SHADES OF GRAY NECKLACE

Four shades of gray are used for the necklace below. To make the color-graded chevrons for this 8-strand braid, I used the following color order: 1 black, 1 dark gray, 1 medium gray, 2 light gray, 1 medium gray, 1 dark gray, 1 black. I increased the size of the 5/2 pearl cotton by twisting strands together to make a larger sized yarn (see How to Make a Twisted Cord, page 102).

CORD IN RED AND BLACK

Two red ends working opposite each other make little chevrons along this black cord. To secure the rubber glasses holders and to secure the ends, I threaded the braid first through silver cones, looped it around the rubber holder, and back through the cone. On one end I clipped the threads flush with the cone; on the other end I cut the ends short and unplied the yarn to make a short fringe.

Project 11

BRAIDED ROPE MATS

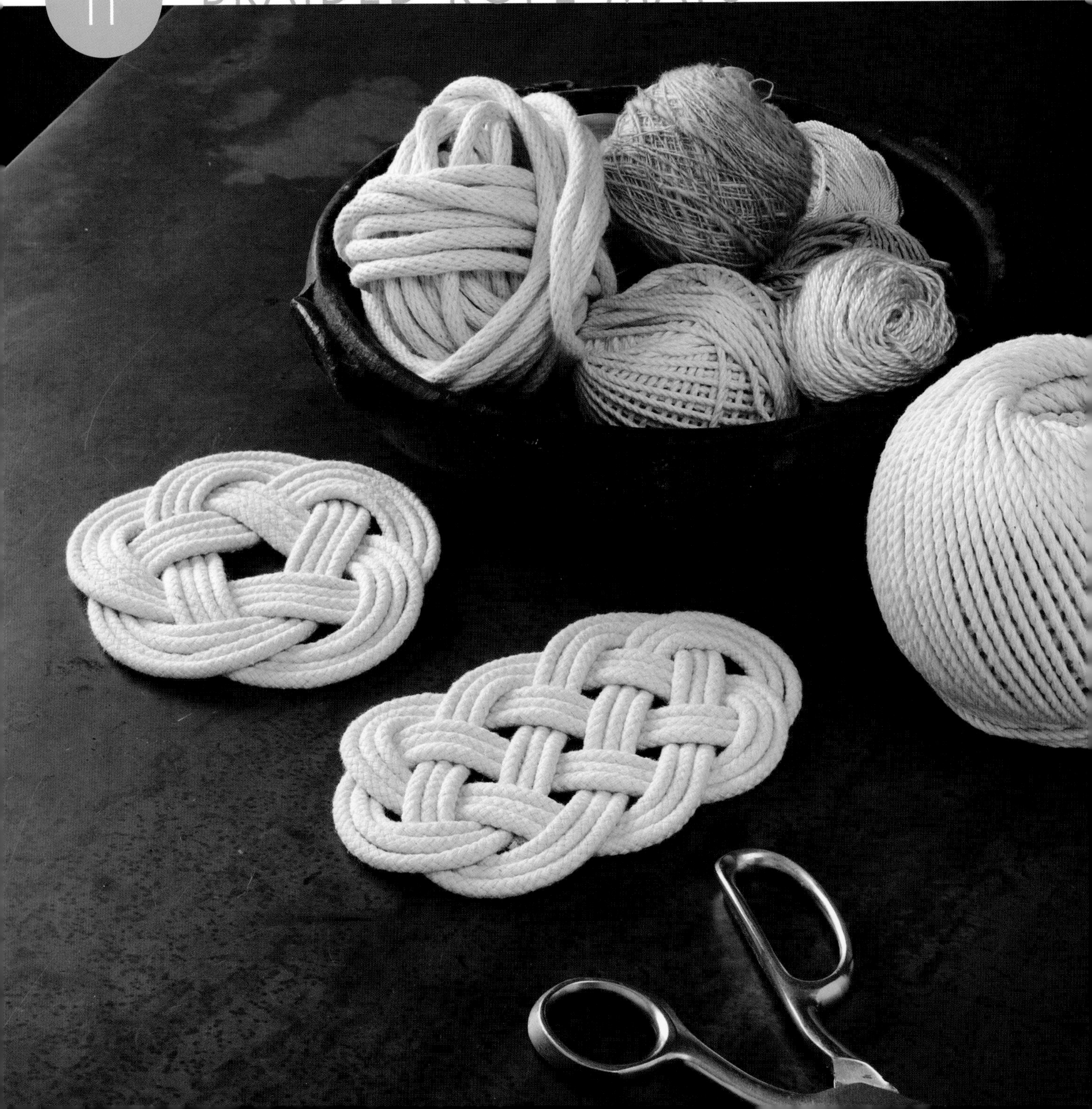

Many of the knots we know today come from life at sea, and with good reason. Knots were critical to life aboard ship, from raising sails to securing lines to anything needing hitching, hoisting, or hauling. Ladders were made from rope and mats were woven as protection against chafing. Simple knots tied up bags and secured parcels, made nets, and attached one thing to another.

Beside the practical side of knots, sailors at sea had time on their hands and plenty of rope. Devising clever ornamental and intricate knot designs helped pass the time and provided a form of entertainment that at times was highly competitive. The secret to a special knot was often carefully kept, only to be shared with one's most trusted mate.

Today we are more likely to fasten things together with a wire twist tie or rubber band. We may know how to tie our shoes, but how many of us know many more knots than that? Knots and braids can be ever so helpful, for hanging a plant, building a garden trellis, making a table mat.

> *"No amount of theoretical knowledge . . . can compensate for*
> *practical experience. Mastering anything takes practice and*
> *tying knots is no exception."*
> —The Book of Decorative Knots *by Peter Owen*

OVERVIEW: These two mats, one woven in *a flat Turk's head* and the other in an ocean braid, are simple once you understand them. Both are woven from cotton-synthetic clothesline and require *only a needle and thread* for binding the ends to prevent fraying and in securing the ends once the mats are woven. For both of these mats, *the basic knot* is made loosely, and then the cord follows *the same path* three or four times to fill in the gaps.

INSTRUCTIONS

MATERIALS AND EQUIPMENT

³⁄₁₆" (5 mm) cotton/synthetic clothesline, 4½ yd (4.2 m) for the Turk's head coaster and 4 yd (3.6 m) for the ocean braid trivet; matching thread or fine yarn; scissors; sewing needle; ruler or tape measure.

RESOURCES

You'll find clothesline at hardware and grocery stores.

FINISHED SIZE

Turk's head coaster—5½" (14 cm) in diameter; ocean braid trivet—4 x 7" (10 x 18 cm).

A NOTE BEFORE YOU BEGIN

Because it is difficult to say in words what you must do, it is important that you study the photographs carefully, comparing what you've done with the photo for each step. Everything matters—if the right end in the photo goes over the left, for example, yours must do the same.

HINTS:

+ *Working on the table is a good way to start. If you have trouble keeping track of the loops, use masking tape to secure them in place as you work.*

+ *Take time to tighten the finished knot—it can take a while, but this is key to the beauty of the finished knot.*

+ *The proportion between rope and braid size is important. If the mat is floppy, tighten it up by increasing the rope size or making the braid smaller.*

+ *These mats take a surprising amount of material. The 7" (180 cm) long trivet requires nearly 4 yards (3.6 m) of rope. To estimate how much you need for a given project, make a dummy knot first to estimate the amount of rope needed.*

TURK'S HEAD COASTER

1 Measure 4½ yd (4.2 m) of rope and wrap the ends to bind them (see How to Wrap Cord, page 82). In the center of the rope make a heart-shaped, 3-cell loop: Holding the right tail and working clockwise, make a full circle motion, bringing the right tail back to the right (see figure a). The right tail should be on top of the loop; the left tail should be under the loop.

2 With the right-hand tail, weave over, under, then over the 3 strands in its path, ending at the top left (see figure b). Pull the yarn through, leaving a loop to create a new cell at the bottom right.

3 With the same end, make a loop to create a new cell across the top, then return to the lower right by weaving under, over, under, then over the 4 strands in its path. There should be pentagon-shaped cell at the center of the knot and every strand should follow an over-under, over-under path (see figure c). You've now completed the full path of the knot.

4 Bring the right-hand tail across the bottom to where the left-hand tail exits the knot, then follow right next to the over-under path of that tail around the knot until you run out of rope. Then use the other tail to follow the path in the other direction until you run out of rope. Follow 1 strand at a time, taking up any slack and adjusting the loops until the knot is even and tidy. When finished, there should be 4 strands of rope throughout and the two tails should end at the same place (see figure d). To finish, bind one tail with sewing thread, stitch across all strands to the other tail, bind this tail with thread, and trim the excess tails. Alternately, you could secure the ends with glue.

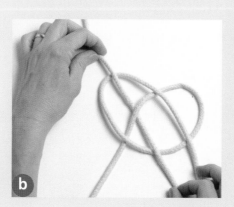

TRIVET

1 Cut 4 yd (3.6 m) of clothesline and bind the ends with thread or fine yarn to prevent raveling (see How to Wrap Cord, page 82). Begin by making a loose overhand knot in the center of the rope: cross the right side over the left, then take the left end through the loop so the right side end is on top of the loop and the left side end is under the loop (see figure a).

2 The next step is a matter of extending the loops of the knots so that the overall length is 7" (18 cm). Adjust the loop so that it has 2 long cells that meet at a smaller triangular cell at the top (see figure b). This sets the outer perimeter of the knot, which will grow inward.

3 Twist (or fold) each long loop to the left so that they cross themselves (figure c).

4 Place the left loop on top of the right loop. You will now have 9 cells. Adjust the loops so that the cells are roughly equal in size (see figure d).

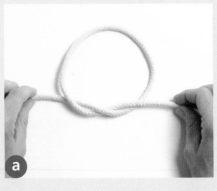

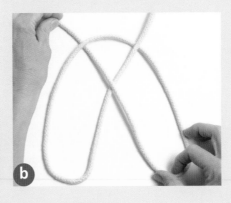

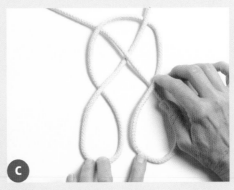

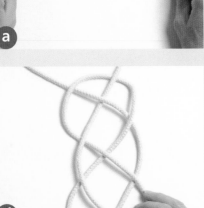

5 Working from upper right to lower left, bring the right-hand tail under the first strand of the loop on the right side edge, then over both of the next 2 strands, and under the strand at the bottom left. Pull the strand through, leaving a small loop to create a new cell at the upper right (see figure e).

6 Working from upper left to lower right, bring the upper left-hand tail over the first strand of the loop on the left side edge, then under, over, under, over the 4 strands on its way to the lower right. If all of the strands cross over, under, over, under, you've set up the knot correctly. Pull the

strand through, leaving a small loop to create a new cell at the upper left, then adjust the strands so that all of the cells are roughly the same size (see figure f).

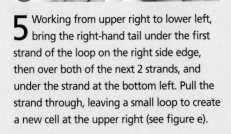

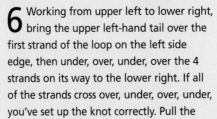

7 Bring the left-hand tail around the bottom to where the right-hand tail comes out of the knot, and follow right next to the over-under path of the right-hand tail, ending up at the lower right corner (see figure g). Next, bring the other tail around the bottom and follow the over-under path already set. Continue to follow the established path (see figure h), tightening up the rope as you go, until there are 3 strands of rope throughout.

8 Adjust the knot until it is tight and uniform. Take up slack as necessary so that the knot is stable, not floppy (see figure i).

9 To finish, bind one tail with sewing thread. Then stitch across all strands in the group to the other tail and bind this tail (see figure j). Trim. Alternately, you could glue the ends to secure them.

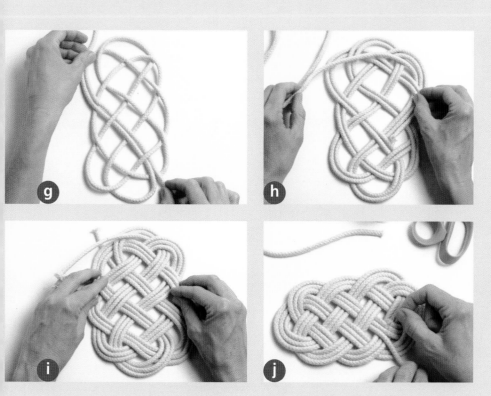

VARIATIONS

INCREASE SIZE

To increase the size of a mat, you can start bigger and increase the number of times you repeat the woven path, up to four times. Or you can increase the size of your cord, or both, which is the case with this variation. I increased the size of the cord—from 3/16" (5 mm) used for the trivet to 1/4" (6 mm), as well as increased the overall length to 8" (20.5 cm). For a denser mat, I added another round, for a total of four with very little space left between the elements.

TECHNIQUES

HOW TO WRAP CORD

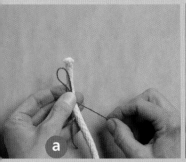

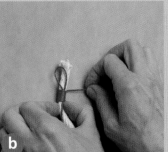

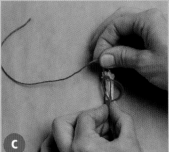

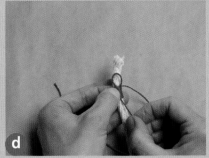

1 Make a loop of the wrapping thread that points towards the end of the rope (see figure a).

2 With the working end and beginning at the end away from the loop, wrap the thread tightly around the rope (see figure b).

3 When you've wrapped for as many times as you want, place the working end through the loop (see figure c).

4 Pull on the short end of the thread to pull the loop snugly down into the wrapped area (see figure d). Trim the thread ends close to the wrap. Trim the ends of the thread.

HAIR TIE

Think small. Using a ⅛" (3 mm) polyester braided cord, I wove a small braid measuring 2 x 3" (5 x 7.5 cm) for a hair tie. A wooden hair pick threaded through the braid is all that's needed to secure it.

SISAL MAT

Create a look by choosing materials carefully. Here, I chose a highly textured sisal rope for a mat with a rustic look and feel. For this mat measuring 7 x 11" (18 x 28 cm), three rounds were used for an open weave.

FURTHER READING

The following sources offer practical instruction on making decorative and useful knots: *The Complete Book of Decorative Knots* by Geoffrey Budworth (The Lyons Press, 1998), *The Book of Decorative Knots* by Peter Owen (Lyons and Burford, 1994), and *The Handbook of Knots* by Des Pawson (DK Publishing, 1998). *The Ashley Book of Knots* (Doubleday, 1944) is a wonderfully and entertaining historical read, encompassing some 3,900 knots.

A well-known author once noted that his success could be attributed to putting in plenty of "chair time." That is, he needed to occupy his writing chair every day and work at something in order to produce results. I found this attitude helpful for two reasons: it took "creativity" off the pedestal and offered encouragement to dedicate the necessary time to get results. Such was the case with the process that brought me to this pillow design.

My initial idea was to weave a pocket with a flap with wide fabric strips, and I became tortured by the fact that I could not make it work. I tried different structures, various sizes of fabric strips and fabrics, and alternative ways of weaving the pocket. I could weave a pocket, but it was structurally unsound and aesthetically sloppy.

I needed to put in some "chair time." I had to let go of an idea and I had to ask the question "what if." In this case, after spending considerable time working on a design solution, the idea of using the actual pillow form as the "loom" for my fabric strips came bubbling up.

I'm telling you this so you'll understand that "creativity" is highly overrated. Ask most any "creative" person, and you'll find that "chair time," not creativity, is the key to their success.

OVERVIEW: This project demonstrates that *a loom can be most anything.* Here, a polyester *pillow form* provides the base for *woven fabric strips.* Undyed cotton canvas is cut into strips, woven over the form, and embellished with *vintage beads.*

INSTRUCTIONS

MATERIALS AND EQUIPMENT

60" (152.2 cm) wide undyed cotton canvas (also called duck cloth), ¾ yd (68.5 m) cut into 1½" (3.8 cm) wide strips; 14" (35.5 cm) square pillow form; matching sewing thread; 3 strands of olive green embroidery floss; twenty-one ⅜" (1 cm) vintage wooden beads; twenty-one 4 mm seed beads; cutting mat; straight edge; rotary cutter or scissors; safety pins; measuring tape; spray starch; iron.

RESOURCES

Most of these materials can be found at fabric and craft stores.

FINISHED SIZE

About 14" (35.5 cm) square.

"Creativity, as has been said, consists largely of rearranging what we know in order to find out what we do not know. Hence, to think creatively, we must be able to look afresh at what we normally take for granted."

—George Kneller

{ ✱ }

HINTS:

+ *Take care in steam pressing and trimming the washed fabric strips.*

+ *Adjust the strips as you go to ensure uniformity.*

1 Using rotary cutter, cut 15 strips of canvas, each measuring 1½" (3.8 cm) wide and 30" (76 cm) long, and cut 2 strips, each measuring 1½" (3.8 cm) wide and 45" (114.5 cm) long (see figure a). Wash the strips vigorously by hand with laundry detergent, let air-dry until they are just slightly damp, then steam-press firmly on the hottest setting. As you press, unravel the edges and trim off any straggling ends to create short, uniform fringe. To stiffen the strips for a crisper look, use spray starch as you press.

2 Wrap 8 strips all the way around the pillow, parallel to each other but not overlapping. Beginning at the center, wind the first warp all the way around the pillow form. Snug up the strip, overlap the ends, and temporarily secure them with a safety pin (see figure b). On the other side of center, wind the second warp alongside the first strip. Wind all 8 strips, 4 on each side of center.

3 Next, weave 7 weft strips perpendicular to the warp all the way around the pillow. Begin the center of the first weft strip in the center of the pillow. Weave over-under, over-under across the front and back. Temporarily secure with a safety pin. Weave the other 6 weft strips in the same way, 3 strips on either side of the center strip (see figure c). Weave the final 2 strips around all four edges of the pillow (see figure d) and secure temporarily with a safety pin.

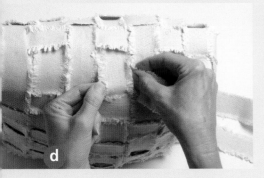

4 When all the strips have been woven, snug up any loose strips and adjust them on the pillow so that they are evenly spaced. The corners may take some extra adjusting. Secure the strips by hand stitching the ends together with sewing needle and thread, adjusting each strip so that the cut ends fall beneath a strip that crosses it, and trimming strips that are too long. Sew across the ends two times using a running stitch.

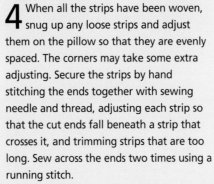

5 The addition of colorful vintage beads turns a tailored design into a whimsical one. I attached ⅜" (1 cm) colored wooden beads with seed beads and embroidery floss (see figure e).

VARIATIONS

STUDY IN PINK

Material and color choice are critical to setting a mood or feeling. For this sweet boudoir pillow in pale pink, the front is accented with sheer and hand-dyed fabric strips woven in simple plain weave. After the ribbons were woven, they were machine stitched to the pillow front before the pillow was sewn.

FURTHER READING

I am always on the lookout for ideas that I translate into weavings. A good source for ideas are periodicals and publications, both those dealing with textile arts, as well as fashion and home décor magazines. Here are some of the magazines I read regularly. Study them as much for color, pattern, and fashion trends as for weaving ideas.

Textile arts: *FiberArts; Handwoven; PieceWork; Selvedge* (British); *Shuttle, Spindle and Dyepot; Spin-Off; Surface Design Journal; Väv Magasinet* (Swedish); *Textileforum* (German).

Fashion: *Cosmopolitan, Elle, Vogue, W.*

Home décor: *Better Homes and Gardens, Country Living, Elle Décor, House Beautiful, Metropolitan Home.*

EMBELLISHMENTS

Just the right button or bead can turn an okay design into a wow. Never turn down a button jar from your mother-in-law or a friend's leftover beads. You just never know when that forgotten button or bead will be the just-right finishing touch for your woven creation. Be on the lookout at auctions and sales. Gems like these are often sold for pennies. From top to bottom: old jewelry, buttons and beads encrusted with rhinestones could dress up a velvet or satin fabric woven pillow; a variety of buttons, such as these reds ones, would add a casual feel to a tailored pillow; vintage rustic beads would be a fun accent for a jean-strip pillow complete with funky embroidery.

POCKET PURSE

If you've ever accidentally washed your wool sweater in the washing machine and discovered with horror that what was once a soft, supple fabric in size 10 is now a stiff, thick, puny size 6, you know what felt is. As you discovered with your sweater, no amount of tugging and pulling will restore it to its former size. Once you've made felt, there's no going back.

Felting uses moisture, heat, and pressure to interlock the scales on the surface of wool fibers. Heat and moisture cause these scales to interlock and become irreversibly entangled.

> *"Those who never made a mistake never made a discovery."*
> *—Samuel Smiles*

OVERVIEW: Two rectangles are loosely woven on a simple frame loom and then machine-washed to *shrink and felt* them. After washing, the rectangles are *hand-sewn together* and finished with a *crocheted handle* and looped trim. This project introduces you to *warping and weaving on a frame loom.*

INSTRUCTIONS

MATERIALS AND EQUIPMENT

2-ply wool in russet at 900 yd/lb (1827 m/kg), 50 yd (46 m) or about 1 ounce (28 g) needed for warp, weft, crochet trim, and handle; sewing needle and matching thread; one 9" (23 cm) stick shuttle; two 9" (23 cm) pick-up sticks; one 6" (15 cm) weaving needle; one size E/4 crochet hook; scissors; sewing needle; weaving frame to weave 6 x 10" (15 x 22.5 cm) at 4 ends per inch (2.5 cm); washing machine and iron for felting and finishing.

WEAVING SPECIFICATIONS

Warp: 23 ends, 4 ends per inch (2.5 cm), 10" (25.5 cm) long.
Weft: 38 picks, 4 ends per inch (2.5 cm), 6" (15 cm) wide.

RESOURCES

Highland 2-ply wool and Peg Loom are from Harrisville Designs. Look for these products at yarn stores that carry weaving supplies.

FINISHED SIZE

About 3½ x 5⅝" (9 x 14 cm), excluding handle.

HINT:

+ *If you notice your weaving drawing in, you are not leaving enough weft yarn in the shed. To correct this, place your weft at an angle to allow more take-up. Also, gently pull out the edge of the weaving when you press the weft into place.*

+ *To help maintain a balanced weave (the same number of warps and wefts per inch), look at the spaces between the threads. If the weave is balanced, these spaces will form squares.*

+ *If you make a mistake, it is best to unweave and correct it right away. If you notice a mistake after removing the fabric from the loom, snip out the errant thread and reweave with a short length of yarn, overlapping it on each side. Leave long tails and clip them after washing.*

1 Weave two rectangles following How to Warp and Weave on a Frame Loom on page 96. Warp loom 6" (15 cm) wide by 10" (22.5 cm) long at 4 warp ends per inch (2.5 cm) for a total of 23 ends (see figure a).

2 Weave a balanced plain weave (the same number of warp and weft threads per inch of weaving) for about 38–40 rows. Weave as close to the pegs as possible. The fabric will be very loose; this is as it should be (see figure b). After you have woven about two-thirds of the way using the pick-up sticks and shuttle, you'll need to switch

to a weaving needle because there won't be room for the pick-up stick or shuttle to pass through. Both rectangles should have an equal number of rows; or they will be different sizes after felting. If there is a little space at the top, adjust the weft spacing so the weaving is even. Uneven weaving will result in uneven finished rectangles.

a

b

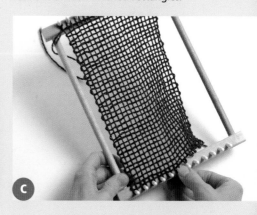

c

d

e

3 Remove the fabric from loom by sliding the loops off the pegs (see figure c). Do not cut the ends. Trim the tails to 2" (5 cm) and leave them hanging.

4 Place the fabric in a large bowl with a generous amount of dish detergent and hot water (see figure d). Agitate the fabric in the soapy water until it begins to shrink and thicken. Then wash the fabric in the washing machine. I've felted my

rectangles in the regular wash cycle with other laundry of like colors. While still damp, steam-press the rectangles, pulling out the edges if necessary so that they are both the same size and have even edges. Trim off the yarn tails.

You can see the felting process progress in these fabric samples at left (see figure e). Sample 1 (left): Unwashed 5¼ x 6¾" (13.5 x 17 cm). Sample 2 (center): Handwashed one minute with Dawn detergent and hot water. Sample measures 4⅜ x 6¼" (11 x 16 cm). Sample 3 (right): Machine washed, hot-cold regular cycle, steam-pressed on hottest setting. Sample measures 3⅝ x 5½" (9 x 14 cm).

5 Place the two rectangles on top of each other and stitch the edges together with matching yarn (see figure f). Begin at one edge and stitch around three sides, leaving a short side open for the top.

6 For the trim, use a size E/4 (3.5 mm) crochet hook to crochet a chain 25" (63.5 cm) long (see How to Crochet a Chain, page 97), forming random loops along the way by working a single crochet into a chain stitch several stitches back from the hook (see figure g). For the handle, crochet a chain 70" (178 cm) long. Tie a knot in the ends of the two crochet chains to secure them during the felting process. Using very soapy hot water, wash the chains until they are felted. They will shrink about 9–10%.

f

g

h

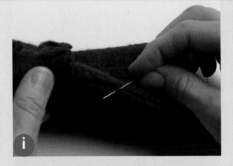

i

7 Using matching thread on a sewing needle, stitch the trim to the top edge of the purse (see figure h), beginning and ending at a seam. Add a second crochet trim to the front, 1½" (3.8 cm) from the upper edge.

8 Leaving a tail about 1¼" (3.2 cm) long extending beyond the bottom corner, stitch the handle to the bag along the side seam, covering the raw edges of the trim (see figure i). Repeat for the other side.

NOTES ON FELTING FABRIC

After it's woven, fabric needs to be washed, or fulled. This process allows the yarn to "bloom" or swell, shrinking the fabric somewhat and filling in the spaces between the yarns. The amount of finishing or fulling depends on the fibers. For example, linen will shrink very little, whereas wool can shrink a lot.

In felting, the fulling properties of wool are taken to the extreme until the fabric is dense and thick. Felting is accomplished with very hot water, agitation, and a generous amount of soap. Machine-washing can make a wool fabric shrink as much as 35% while becoming thick and soft. It's a good idea to check your fabric often to make sure it is not shrinking too much. After felting, you can influence the shape of your rectangle somewhat by pulling on the edges to even them out and pressing them with steam, pressure, and high heat.

TECHNIQUES

HOW TO MAKE A SLIPKNOT

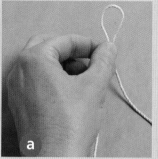 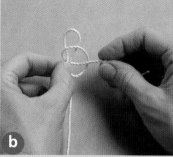 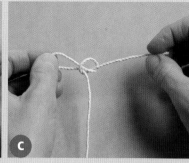 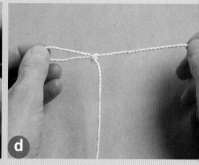

a   b   c   d

1 Make a loop about 6" (15 cm) from the end of the string (see figure a).

2 Encircle the loop with the tail end and slip the tail through this loop (see figure b).

3 Hold the first loop and tail end (see figure c) and pull to tighten (see figure d). The slipknot can be tightened or loosened by pulling on the working end.

HOW TO WIND A SHUTTLE

 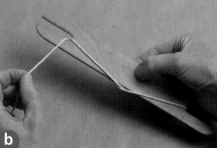 

a   b   c

1 Wind yarn from the front side on one end to the back of the other end of the shuttle (see figure a).

2 Take the yarn from back around the front on the other side. You have now made a figure eight (see figure b).

3 Keep winding in this way to fill this side of the shuttle (see figure c). You can also wind a figure eight on the other side if more yarn on the shuttle is desired.

FURTHER READING

Here are a few resources for learning more about felt. Beverly Gordon's book, *Feltmaking: Traditions, Techniques, and Contemporary Explorations* (Watson-Guptill Publications, 1980) includes solid historical information as well as contemporary examples—good for learning about felting more in depth. *Simply Felt* (Interweave Press, 2004) is full of felted projects—loads of great ideas in this volume. You'll find fun, imaginative projects in these two books: *Feltmaking: Fabulous Wearable, Jewelry, and Home Accents* (The Crowood Press, 2000) and *The Art of Feltmaking* (Watson-Guptill Publications, 1997).

TECHNIQUES

HOW TO WARP AND WEAVE ON A FRAME LOOM

1 Attach the warp to the outermost peg of the loom with a slipknot (see How to Make a Slipknot, page 95). Wind back and forth between the pegs until the desired number of warp ends has been wound (see figure a). Secure by tying the end and cutting off the yarn. Wind a small, flat shuttle with yarn (see How to Wind a Shuttle, page 95).

2 Insert a pick-up (or shed) stick by weaving over, under, over, under all the way across the warp (see figure b). Push this stick up to the top of loom. Stand the pick-up stick on edge to raise every other warp thread and make an opening, or shed, between the alternate threads.

3 Insert the shuttle into the shed (see figure c), leaving a tail of yarn hanging at the edge (it will be cut off or woven in later). Pull the shuttle out the other side, leaving a strand of yarn (weft) behind as you go.

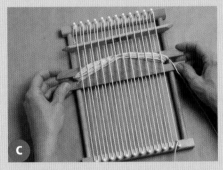

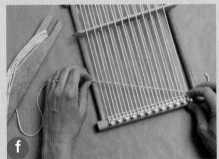

4 Press the weft into place by sliding the pick-up stick down against the weft and pressing it as firmly as possible against the pegs. You have now woven one pick, or row. Slide the pick-up stick up to the top of the loom until it is needed again.

5 To make a shed for the second row, you'll need to use the second pick-up stick to pick up every thread that was not picked up by the first pick-up stick (see figure d). Stand this pick-up stick on edge, insert the shuttle into the shed, and weave back across to the other side.

6 Push this row into place with the pick-up stick (see figure e) and then remove the second pick-up stick (the first pick-up stick remains in place between the warp threads).

7 To help prevent the warp threads from pulling in at the edges, insert the weft at an angle (see figure f). It should be snug against the edge warp but not pull in nor leave a loop weft at the edge.

A balanced weave has an equal number of wefts and warps in an inch. To check your weaving, look at the space between the intersections. In a balanced weave, the spaces between the yarns should form small squares.

HOW TO CROCHET A CHAIN

1 Make a slipknot (see figure a).

2 Place the hook through the slipknot loop and grasp the yarn with the hook (see figure b).

3 Slide the hook with yarn through the first loop. Repeat to make a continuous chain (see figure c).

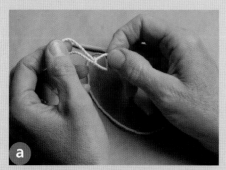

a

b

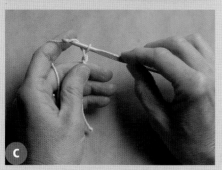

c

VARIATIONS

HOUNDSTOOTH PLAID BAG

This small clutch is made from three rectangles. Two are used to make the bag and a third one forms the flap. To make the houndstooth plaid, two ends of orange and blue are alternated in warp and weft, forming the characteristic pinwheel design. A carved bone bead threaded with yarn adds a decorative accent.

CELL PHONE AT THE READY

Take your cell phone along to a party in this attractive bag with a braided doubled wrist strap. Two solid blue rectangles make up the bag; the solid orange rectangle is cut and applied asymmetrically, edged with a crochet trim, and accented with a pearl button closure.

n weaving, what happens when one hue crosses another is almost always unpredictable. You can think of colored yarns woven across each other as a kind of pointillism because when warp and weft cross, dots of color appear and mingle on the surface.

The simplest way to mix colored yarns is to start with a solid warp in one color and cross it with a different color in the weft. Look up close, then from a distance, and see how your eye mixes the two together.

You can also put more than one color in the warp. If, for example, you alternate two warp ends of green and two ends of blue, you'll have made a striped warp. If you cross the striped warp with stripes of blue and green in the weft, then you'll have woven a simple plaid. Change weft color order, such as weaving three picks of green and three picks of blue, or three picks of green and one of blue, and you'll have a totally different look. Just think of what might happen if you increased your weft stripes to three ends, or four ends, or added a third color. Or use three colors in the warp and three different ones in the weft—the possibilities are virtually limitless, and always full of surprises.

"In our own era of sophisticated technology where we are able to use machines to manufacture mass materials with great speed and ease, there also exists
the desire to make or seek out the unique, the one-of-a-kind,
as an assertion of our own individuality."
—*Jane Redman*, Frame-Loom Weaving

OVERVIEW: This project explores a *simple color idea.* Two colors are alternated in the warp and crossed with *a single weft color.* The resulting fabric has *subtle dots.* The fabric has been washed vigorously to *felt it,* creating a thick, *insulating fabric.*

INSTRUCTIONS

MATERIALS AND EQUIPMENT

For four egg hats (two fabric squares): warp, weft, and trim: Harrisville Designs Shetland 2-ply wool at 1800 yd/lb (3654 m/kg), 160 yd (146 m) dark green Cypress, 52 yd (48 m) light green Tundra, and 6 yd (5.5 m) Rose. It's important to choose a 100% wool yarn that will shrink when washed. You'll also need an ounce of yellow, orange, red, and blue wool fleece for the bird; Schacht School Loom, or 15 x 21" (38 x 53.5 cm) frame with nails or pegs set at about 5.5 per inch (2.5 cm); one stick shuttle; two pick-up sticks; one 6" (15 cm) weaving needle; tailor's chalk; felting needle; foam pad; scissors; sewing needle and thread; measuring tape; paper pattern.

RESOURCES

Most of these supplies are available at weaving shops.

FINISHED SIZE

About 4 x 2 x 2" (10 x 5 x 5 cm), without felted chick.

HINTS:

+ *When weaving with more than one color, put as many of the color changes as possible in the warp. For example, I alternated two colors in the warp for the egg hats, instead of using them in the weft where two shuttles would be required, making the weaving go more slowly.*

+ *To increase the tension on the warp, start on the edge and pull up yarns sequentially across the warp to take up extra slack. Work first one color and then the other. Pat the warp to determine if one side is tighter or looser than the other and adjust accordingly. Theoretically, because the warp is a continuous strand of yarn, the tension should even itself out. Practice has shown, however, that adjusting the tension as described above makes a more even warp.*

+ *To catch the edge thread when alternating two shuttles, keep these rules in mind: when the first shuttle passes over the selvedge thread, place it away from you and the second shuttle near you. When the first shuttle passes under the selvedge thread, place it closest to you and the following shuttle away from you.*

1 For complete warping and weaving instructions, see How to Warp and Weave on a Frame Loom on page 96. Alternating 1 strand each of Cypress and Tundra, warp the entire width of the frame, or 15" (38 cm) wide, for a total of 83 warp ends spaced at about 5.5 ends per inch (2.5 cm). One fabric square will make two egg hats.

2 Use Cypress for weft and weave a simple over-under plain weave with the same number of wefts per inch as warps per inch. Fill the entire frame with weaving, switching to a needle when it is no longer possible to get the shuttle through.

3 Remove the fabric from the loom (see figure b) and wash by hand to partially felt the fabric. Then machine wash in hot water with other laundry of like colors, checking often to see that the fabric is sufficiently felted (see figure c). Remove from the washer when the fabric measures 8 x 10¼" (20.5 x 26 cm). Lay flat to dry and steam press.

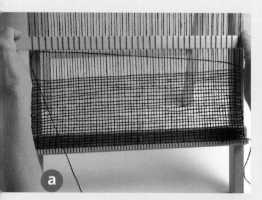

a

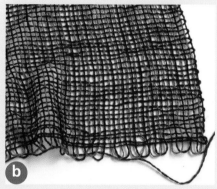

b

c

d

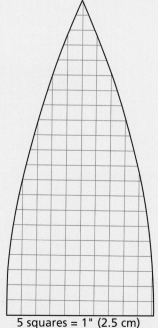

e

4 Cut out a paper pattern from the template at right. For each egg hat, cut 4 shapes (you'll be able to cut 8 shapes from the felted fabric). I traced the shape with tailor's chalk (see figure d) and then cut out the pieces.

5 squares = 1" (2.5 cm)

5 Place 2 pieces together and use a sewing needle and thread to stitch them together. I used the weave pattern as a sewing guide, stitching 1 square in from the edge and making each stitch 1 square long. Pull the thread tight after each stitch. Stitch from the bottom edge up to the top, stopping about ¾" (2 cm) from the top edge. Repeat for the other pieces.

6 For each egg hat, measure 3 lengths of yarn, each 27" (68.5 cm) long. Follow the instructions for How to Make a Twisted Cord, below, to make a twisted cord 24" (61 cm) long.

7 Wrap sewing thread around the cord to secure the end, leaving about a ³⁄₁₆" (5 mm) tassel at the end (see figure f). Stitch the cord along the center of each seam, catching just the underside with a needle and thread (see figure g). Stitch up to the

point and make a loop about ½" (1.3 cm) long and wrap with sewing thread. Stitch down other side and wrap cord as before. Repeat for the opposite side.

8 To trim the remaining 2 points, wrap one end of the remaining cord with sewing thread, secure the cord to the wrong side in the gap between 2 points, then stitch it to the edge of the fabric. Stitch up to the point, make a loop and wrap with sewing thread as you did before,

then stitch down to the valley on the other side. Wrap the end of the cord with sewing thread and secure it to the wrong side of the hat. Repeat for the remaining point.

9 Cut the center of the ½" (1.3) loops, then use a needle to ravel the yarn to make small tassels (see figure h). Trim the tassels to even lengths. Make felted bird and securely stitch to top of egg hat (see How to Make a Needle-Felted Bird, page 103).

TECHNIQUES

HOW TO MAKE A TWISTED CORD

To make a twisted cord, or fringe, you need at least two yarns or groups of yarn. For this example I used two single yarns. Step one: twist the yarns separately in the same direction (see figure a). Twist in the same direction that the yarn is spun so that it gets tighter and begins to kink on itself. Step two: lay the yarns side by side without letting go of them and twist them together in the opposite direction (see figure b). Tie an overhand knot in the end so the cord can't untwist.

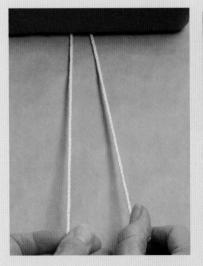

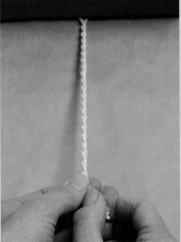

TECHNIQUES

HOW TO MAKE A NEEDLE-FELTED BIRD

You can felt wool by just stabbing it repeatedly with a special barbed needle. The needle used here is available at yarn stores that carry felting materials. I purchased about an ounce of commercially dyed fiber to make the bird. Hold the fleece against the foam pad while working it with the felting needle. Be careful not to stab yourself!

1 For a multicolored effect blend orange and yellow fleece by gently pulling the fiber apart and layering the two colors one on top of the other. Keep pulling and overlaying until the colors are blended (see figure a).

2 Roll a square of fleece about 2 x 3" (5 x 7.5 cm) from the short side. Begin shaping bird by needle-felting a line across the top from front to back to define the head (see figure b).

3 Gently pull some fiber out of the tail end and needle-felt it to flatten, coaxing in the edges to make a pointed tail (see figure c).

4 Needle-felt all over to compress the body. Lift up the tail and needle-felt heavily with many stabs until it stands up by itself (see figure d).

5 For head, needle-felt in a circle to establish the general shape (see figure e). Press down on the top of the head and needle-felt through the head into body to secure it in place. Work around head, needling where any shaping

is needed. Lift up on head and needle the neck area to smooth the chest. Needle down the center back to establish an impression of folded wings. Keep felting where any shaping is needed.

6 For eyes, take a tiny piece of blue fleece and gently press it into the side head. When it is partially secured, needle through the eye to make a small depression for an eye socket (see figure f). Repeat for other side.

7 For bill, tear off a small piece of red fleece and form it into a triangle. Needle-felt flat on your foam form. When it is stiff, attach it to the head, needling through the bill into the head until secure. Securely stitch bird to top of egg hat.

TECHNIQUES

HOW TO MAKE AND USE STRING HEDDLES

Weaving is much faster and easier if you don't have to weave over-under, over-under every warp. A simple way to streamline the process is to use a shed stick and string heddles. Here's how it works: with a broad, flat, smooth stick, weave over and under alternate warp ends. When you turn this stick on edge, it will automatically raise half the warp ends so you can pass the shuttle through easily. This shed stick stays in place throughout the weaving process. To raise the other warp ends, loop around each of them with a string loop, or heddle. When you lift these loops, those warps will be raised so you can insert a second shed stick. It will hold the shed open long enough to pass the shuttle through, and then will be removed until it is needed again.

1 Make a template for tying the heddles: 4" (10 cm) wide mat board was used here (see figure a). Cut strong string such as cotton carpet warp at least 6" (15 cm) long. Tie over the edge of the template with a square knot (right over left, left over right) to make a loop. Trim the ends short.

2 After all the heddles have been made, slide one under each warp end that is not on the pick-up stick (see figure b).

a

b

c

d

3 Slide each string heddle onto a heddle stick that is long enough to extend past the edge of the weaving and grasp with your hands (see figure c).

4 To keep heddles in place, cover them with masking tape. To weave, lift up on the heddle stick (which lifts the warps) and slide in the second pick-up stick and turn on edge to make the shed (see figure d).

FURTHER READING

Felted fabric and needle felting have been explored here, but there are other ways to make felt, such as felting raw fiber with soap and water or felting knitted fabrics. Fortunately, several felting books are available, filled with useful and fun ideas. Two of my favorites are *Simply Felt* by Margaret Docherty and Jayne Emerson (Interweave Press, 2004) and *Felted Knits* by

Beverly Galeskas (Interweave Press, 2003). Both provide basic felting information and easy, appealing projects. If you get into felted figures, check out the aptly named *Felt Wee Folk: Enchanting Projects* by Sally Mayor (C&T Publishing, 2003). You can't get much cuter than this.

Two excellent books featuring color-and-weave samples are written by Ann Sutton. *The Structure of Weaving* (Lark Books, 1982) is about understanding weave structure and fabric design. Basic information is provided as well as idea-filled woven examples, including a color-and-weave sampler that could be fodder for an entire weaving career. Taking color-and-weave even further is her *Color-and-Weave Design Book: A Practical Reference Book* (Lark Books, 1984), which is completely devoted to this phenomenon.

VARIATIONS

COLOR-AND-WEAVE

Interesting things happen when different color sequences in a warp are crossed with other color sequences in the weft. The simplest example is a check: even stripes in the warp woven with even stripes in the weft. But that is just the beginning of the possibilities that weavers refer to as "color-and-weave effect." Try a few samples and you'll begin to appreciate the variations. Here are a few examples to get you started, from left to right beginning with the top row.

Sample 1: Dots on a background
Warp: All dark green
Weft: 1 light green, 1 dark green

Sample 2: Stripes. Note: One face will have vertical stripes and the other horizontal.
Warp: 1 dark green, 1 light green
Weft: 1 dark green, 1 light green

Sample 3: A traditional herringbone pattern
Warp: 2 dark green, 2 light green
Weft: 2 dark green, 2 light green

Sample 4: Hatching
Warp: 2 dark green, 1 light green
Weft: 2 dark green, 1 light green

Sample 5: Stripes and dots
Warp: 1 dark green, 3 light green
Weft: 1 dark green, 3 light green

Sample 6: Check plaid
Warp: 4 dark green, 4 light green
Weft: 4 dark green, 4 light green

Sample 7: Stripes and crosses
Warp: 2 dark green, 1 light green
Weft: 1 dark green, 1 light

PILE PATCH

Weft-faced fabrics are those in which the weft completely covers the warp. The weft is usually heavier than the warp, and the warp threads are widely spaced so the weft can be packed in tightly. Traditionally, weft-faced weaves were thick and sturdy fabrics, originally used in doorways and along walls to provide warmth. Huge tapestries, such as the well-known unicorn tapestries, provided beauty to a room, but their original purpose was to warm a cold and drafty hall. Likewise, heavy pile hangings, known in Scandinavia as rya rugs, traditionally hung in doorways or anywhere protection was needed from the cold. In the East, where rug weaving reached a high art, rugs were the take-along answer to warmth and comfort for a nomadic people.

Today, rugs are as likely to be found on the floor as they are on the wall, lending softness underfoot and warmth to the room through texture and color. Though mass-produced rugs are the norm, there continue to be places where rugs are woven using methods unchanged for centuries.

Weft-faced rugs fall into two main categories, flat weave and pile. Flat-weave rugs may encompass selvedge-to-selvedge weaving and tapestry, in which many wefts travel short distances to weave a design (discontinuous wefts). Pile weaves most often are comprised of a plain-weave ground and a supplementary pile, which might be looped or knotted. The plain-weave ground provides stability; the pile technique is used for patterning.

This pile patch introduces flat and pile rug weaves. The end borders are flat weave, the fringe is rya knotting, and the center is looping with a plain-weave ground.

OVERVIEW: Weft-faced *rug techniques* are used to make this *monogram patch.* The warp is threaded wide enough to accommodate a *soft, squishy, wool* yarn that completely covers the warp. Woven on a *small frame loom,* this project is one that can be *taken along* on vacation or in the soccer carpool.

INSTRUCTIONS

MATERIALS AND EQUIPMENT

Warp: Maysville cotton carpet warp at 1600/yd/lb (3245 m/kg), 25 yd (23 m) #7 red-brown;

Weft: Brown Sheep Lamb's Pride wool singles (85% wool, 15% mohair) at 760 yd/lb (1545 m/kg), 15 yd (14 m) M-180 Ruby Red, 12 yd (11 m) M-97 Rust, 2 yd (2 m) each of M-67 Loden Leaf and M-14 Sunburst Gold, and 6 yd (5.5 m) M-89 Roasted Coffee; Schacht Mini Loom or weaving frame to accommodate 4½ x 8½" (11 x 24 cm) and 7 ends per inch (2.5 cm); two small shuttles; one size 10 (6 mm) knitting needle; one small beater or fork; 6" (15 cm) weaving needle; tapestry needle; pick-up stick; fabric glue; glue stick; scissors; cuticle or similar small scissors; tape measure.

RESOURCES

The cotton carpet warp is Maysville Carpet Warp from January and Wood Co.; the wools singles are Lamb's Pride from Brown Sheep; the frame loom is the Mini Loom from Schacht Spindle Co. Inc. All are available from yarn and/or weaving stores.

FINISHED SIZE

About 4½ x 6½" (11.5 x 16.5 cm), including fringe.

HINTS:

+ *To keep the sides from pulling in, allow extra yarn in the shed. Placing the yarn at an angle and then beating the weft down on a closed shed will help keep the weft firmly in place.*

+ *When picking up loops on the knitting needle, always start on the side from which the yarn has been inserted into the shed.*

+ *After every inch or so of weaving, press down firmly all across the top of the weaving to pack in the weft.*

1 Using cotton carpet warp, measure 29 ends, each 8½" (21.5 cm) long (see How to Warp and Weave on a Frame Loom, page 96). Double the cotton carpet warp and twine across two times (see How to Twine, page 23), 1½" (3.8 cm) from bottom of frame. Weave ½" (1.3 cm) with cotton carpet warp for hem (see figure a). Press the weft into place so that it completely covers the warp. Cut off yarn and tuck end back into the weaving.

2 Using red yarn, wind a butterfly (see How to Wind a Butterfly, page 23), tuck in the end at the selvedge (avoid bulk by splitting the tail, so it's half the thickness, before tucking it in), and weave two rows (or picks). Make a row of red ghiordes knots (see How to Make a Ghiordes or Rya Knot, page 111; I used 6" [15 cm] lengths for the knots), weave two rows of plain weave, then make another row of knots for a total of two rows of knots (see figure b). Finally, weave two rows of plain weave. Cut off the red yarn and tuck in the tail. Alternate 2 picks each of green and yellow, beginning and ending with green, for a total of 5 stripes.

3 Wind two shuttles, one with orange yarn and the other with brown. Beginning with brown, alternate 1 pick each of these two colors for the duration of the monogram area. Weave 5 picks. On the 6th (orange) pick, use the knitting needle (see figure c) to make loops (see How to Make a Looped Pile, page 111) following a letter of the alphabet on page 112. (Note: On an open shed, there are 13 spaces that correspond to the diagram; alternate orange and brown for a total of 6 picks for each square in the diagram.) Pick up loops on the orange picks. When you've finished the monogram, weave the border in the reverse order used in Step 2. Begin with 5 picks alternating orange and brown. Alternate 2 picks each of green and yellow for 5 stripes, ending with red ghiordes knots, hem and twining (see figure d). You want to pack the weft in very tightly, covering the warp completely (see figure e).

4 Remove weaving from loom and secure ends with overhand knots. Sew any loose ends into the weaving. Trim all ends. Before cutting the loops, paint the back of the patch with fabric glue to secure the cut loops (see figure f).

5 Cut ghiordes knots to 1¼" (3.2 cm). Cut monogram loops very short, about ³⁄₁₆" (5 mm) long (see figure g). After cutting, rub the fringe in every direction to check for uneven areas. Trim until the surface is uniform and pleasingly fuzzy. Fold under hems and stitch the patch to a pillow.

" . . . Psychologists tell us that our closest sensations of reality come through the sense of touch. We are all aware that things we see may not be actual, and the things we hear may be illusions, but we never for an instant doubt the reality of the things we touch."

—Mary Atwater, Byways in Handweaving

TECHNIQUES

HOW TO MAKE A GHIORDES OR RYA KNOT

1 Make a gauge, such as a file card or piece of mat board to cut yarn to uniform lengths (see figure a). I find 6" (15 cm) lengths comfortable to work with.

2 On a closed shed, place a length of yarn around two warp ends (see figure b).

3 Hold the ends together in one hand and with the other hand separate the two warp ends and pull a loop of yarn through the center of the two warp ends. Pull the ends of the yarn through the lifted loop (see figure c).

4 Pull down knot to tighten (see figure d). Weave at least two rows of plain weave (also called ground weave) before beginning the next row of knots.

HOW TO MAKE A LOOPED PILE

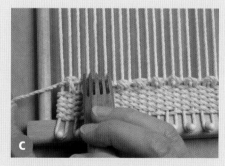

1 Looped pile is made by picking up weft loops. Insert weft yarn into the shed and snug it up against the edge of the weaving as usual. Then use a knitting needle to pick up loops as desired, beginning at the edge where the yarn enters the shed and bringing up slack from the loose weft in the shed (see figure a).

2 Weave one or two rows of plain weave between the rows of looped wefts. It is important to pack the weft in tightly so the loops do not pull out (see figure b). I like to leave the knitting needle in place until after the next row of plain weave has been woven. Slide the knitting needle out and then press the weft firmly down against the loops.

3 The loops are most secure if each row of loops is followed by two rows of plain weave (see figure c); if only one row of plain weave is worked between loops, it may be necessary to glue the back of the weaving as further security. Use a flexible fabric glue. For cut pile, cut the loops after weaving.

VARIATIONS

PILE HEART

Overall pile was woven for this petite pillow patch. The ground weft is completely hidden by the knotted surface. Cutting the knots short helps reveal the overall design on this small weaving. Pillow design by Louise Bradley.

THE ALPHABET

Use the graphed alphabet below for your own custom pile patch. Each square equals the space between two raised warps where the loop will be pulled to the surface and three rows of weft loops (or 6 picks—3 picks of plain weave and 3 picks of loops). The number of weft loops required to "square" the design will vary according to the size of the yarn being used. Adjust the number of loop rows accordingly.

RYA OR GHIORDES KNOT SAMPLER

Ghiordes knots, or rya, are knots made on a plain-weave, weft-faced fabric (left). Because each knot is tied individually, many design and color options are possible. Usually the best way to design a project is to determine the number of spaces between warps and then draw your design on graph paper before taking it to the loom. This sampler explores some of the possibilities, from bottom to top: pile spots on a plain-weave background, different lengths of cut pile, allover pile. Designed and woven by Suzanne Najarian.

LOOP PILE

Loop pile is faster to weave than ghiordes knots, but it does not offer as much design freedom. Loop pile does offer many textural possibilities, as explored here (above right): cut and uncut pile, small and large loops, single and multicolored textures. Consider using loop pile for trimming a design, as well as for allover texture.

FURTHER READING

The "Bible" of rug weaving, *The Techniques of Rug Weaving* by Peter Collingwood (Watson-Guptill Publications, 1972) continues to be my "go to" source on any rug technique I need to know about. I have yet to be disappointed. Though it's been around for a while, Shirley Held's *Weaving: A Handbook for Fiber Craftsman* (Holt Rinehart and Winston, 1973) is still used as a textbook in university weaving programs. It covers a broad spectrum of weaving techniques and includes historical information along with good descriptions of many weave structures. In addition, Jane Redman's *Frame-Loom Weaving* (Van Nostrand Reinhold, 1976) offers good line drawings and how-tos on many hand-manipulated weaves.

Project 15

FUZZY COLLAR

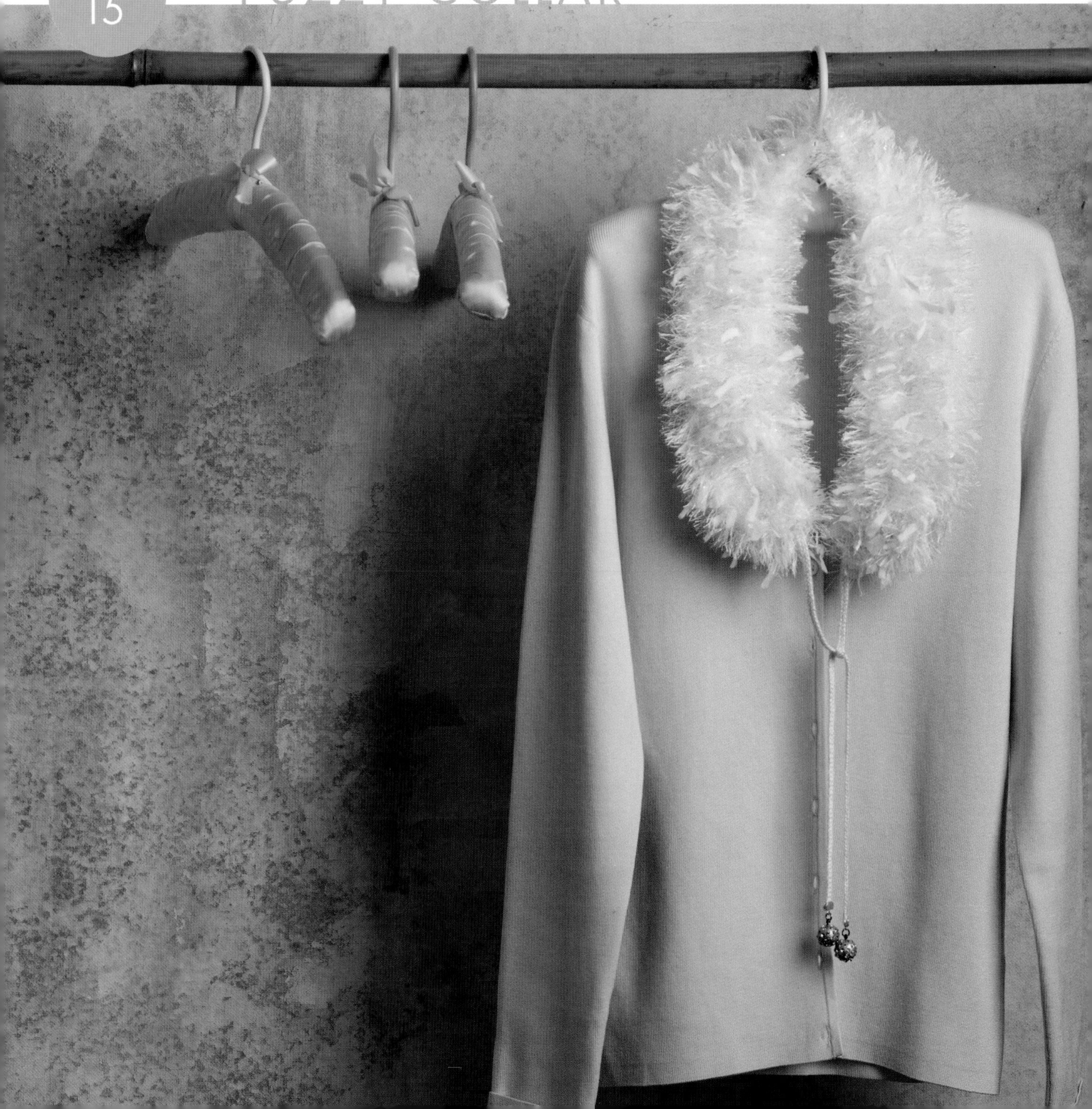

Yarn is the bones of weaving. As warp it is the skeleton that the weft binds to, to create whole cloth. The nature of the fabric depends on several elements: yarn, color, interlacement, finishing. Usually cloth begins with yarn.

Sometimes a project is inspired by the yarn—sometimes it's just too hard to resist a luscious yarn—and you begin a project by asking, "what can I make with this yarn?" Other times a project begins with an idea of what you want to make, and then you choose the yarns. This latter approach is probably the prudent way to begin, but I've done both ways. My yarn stash by this time is considerable, though I rarely purchase yarn on impulse these days.

Don't get me wrong. A yarn stash is a very good thing. It is a ready supply of material and helpful for sampling ideas. If truth were known, sampling is where my weaving heart and soul lie. In sampling I try out ideas that give me more ideas. For me, sampling is the creative part of weaving that I most love. Making a sample, or several samples, will almost always tell me what I need to know. I end up with something that works, instead of something that will be relegated to the bottom drawer.

A wise friend once said, "The mistake is in the beginning." Henning was referring to life issues in general, but I find this phrase running around in my head quite often as I work out a design. If I don't choose the right yarn or effective color combination, then the piece is wrong before I ever begin. The mistake is in the beginning. Sampling first avoids many a misguided project.

OVERVIEW: Making this Fuzzy Collar is so simple it's like *child's play,* using a weaving technique usually practiced by school children. A set of ordinary drinking straws (though in this case I used more grown-up aluminum tubes) are *threaded* with warp yarn to provide a rigid base for weaving. The weft passes over and under the straws or tubes, and as *the fabric grows,* it is simply pushed down onto the *warp yarn dangling* below the tubes until the desired length is achieved.

INSTRUCTIONS

MATERIALS AND EQUIPMENT

Warp: DMC #5 perle cotton at 2100 yd/lb in bleached white, 14 yd (13 m) needed.

Weft: 35 yd (32 m) of each of the following yarns: Crystal Palace Fling, nylon-lurex novelty at 1180 yd/lb (2395 m/kg) in white #3687; Erdal Eyelash Tweed polyester novelty at 360 yd/lb (730 m/kg) in white #1; Berroco Sizzle Bright polyester-nylon at 840 yd/lb (1963 m/kg) in white #1688; Cotton Clouds 3310 Chenille viscose chenille at 1300 yd/lb (2639 m/kg) in #010 Bleach (all weft yarns are used together as one; feel free to substitute any textured novelty yarns you have on hand—just about any fuzzy yarn will work); two ⅜" (1 cm) ribbon crimps; two split rings; two ½" (1.3 cm) spherical antique buttons; 6" (15 cm) weaving needle; scissors; ⅛" (3 mm) diameter, 36" (91.5 cm) long aluminum tube cut into seven 5" (12.5 cm) lengths; masking tape; tape measure; weight; needle-nose pliers wrapped with masking tape; sandpaper.

"The weaver who dies with the most yarn wins."
—Anita Luvera Mayer

RESOURCES

Look for these yarns at knitting and weaving stores as well as through mail-order yarn companies. The findings can be found at bead and craft stores. Look for decorative buttons at antique and fine fabric stores.

FINISHED SIZE

Collar—2½ x 26" (6.5 x 66 cm); ties—each 11" (28 cm) long.

HINTS:

+ *You must have an odd number of warps for this technique.*

+ *Consider the number of tubes you can comfortably hold in your hands. I found nine to be the limit of what I could manage.*

+ *Fuzzy yarns mask the bulky appearance of this weaving technique.*

+ *This is a great way to use leftover yarns; three to five yarns in a variety of textures and colors make a rich, densely textured surface.*

1 Measure and mark seven 5" (12.5 cm) lengths on the aluminum tube. Score with a knife or saw along the marks, and then break off each section. Use sandpaper to smooth any rough edges. Alternately, you can use ordinary drinking straws, though they are bigger in diameter and less rigid than the aluminum tubing. For the warp, cut seven 2 yd (1.8 m) lengths of perle cotton. Using the needle, thread each warp through a tube and secure one end to the tube with masking tape (see figure a). Tie the other ends of the warp together in a single overhand knot.

2 Use all four weft yarns as one. Tie them to an outside tube with a slipknot (see How to Make a Slipknot, page 95). Hold the tubes like a deck of cards in one hand (see figure b). With the other hand, weave over-under, over-under, back and forth across the tubes. As the weft builds up on the tubes, push it down onto the cotton warp.

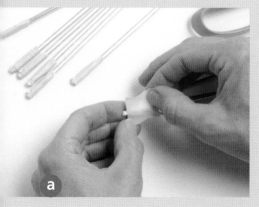

3 Pack the weaving firmly, at about 15 picks per inch (2.5 cm). Adjust the density of the weaving by holding one end and sliding the weaving along the warp (see figure c). Continue weaving until the collar measures 26" (66 cm). Cut off the weft, leaving a 6" (15 cm) tail, and secure the tail to an edge warp with a slipknot.

4 Slide the weaving down the warp (see figure d) until there are about 21" (53.5 cm) of warp length at each end of the collar.

5 Shape the collar by pulling both ends of the warp yarn along one edge of the woven piece, crowding the wefts along that side, until the desired curved shape is achieved (see figure e). Tie over-hand knots to secure the warp ends as close to the weaving as possible.

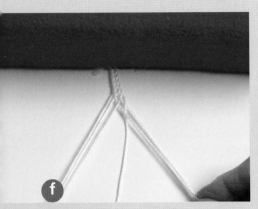

6 For ties, you will use the perle cotton warps still attached to the collar. Use the warps at each end of the collar to make a 7-strand flat braid in the same manner as the 9-strand braid on page 68, weaving over 2, under 1 (see figure f). Work until the braids measure 11" (28 cm) long. Trim ends. If fraying is a problem, place a dot of glue to secure the ends of the braids before attaching the buttons.

7 Attach the spherical buttons to the braid crimps with split rings. Use the wrapped pliers to clamp the braid crimp securely to the end of the braid (see figure g).

ALL ABOUT YARN
Contrast and color are the key to the appeal of these fun belts. The yellow belt combines a ribbon yarn with a fine, fuzzy orange yarn, a blue-and-white yarn, and a spiky white novelty yarn. For the second belt, a blue and red variegated ribbon yarn is highlighted by a bright red ribbon and a fine, fuzzy, bright blue yarn. The caterpillar-like effect in the third belt is achieved by combining a black-and-white ribbon yarn with a long white eyelash yarn. Notice the dark accent at the beginning of the belt where just the ribbon yarn was used.

VARIATIONS

SHAG COLLAR

Three fine eyelash yarns combine to make this mutlicolored and textured collar (right). Matching antique rhinestone broaches accent the ends.

RHINESTONE BUCKLE BELT

Non-fuzzy but textured yarns are used for this belt accented with rhinestone buttons and buckle (below). A rich quality is achieve by combining three different yarns close in hue and texture.

WRISTLET

Elastic is the warp for this warm, decorative cuff (above right). Two colors of rayon chenille plus a beige eyelash and a brown-tone novelty yarn create a furry cuff with textural accents. After weaving, the elastic ends are tied together and then stitched to safely secure the knots.

FURTHER READING

I am of the opinion that there's never too much art and craft in kids' lives. Kids love to get their hands on things. For them, especially at a young age, it's as much about the process as it is about the finished product. I encourage you to make materials available to kids and let them just play. As they get older, they will care more about the finished product and that will be a good time to provide better-quality materials and further instruction. Two books with the same title, *Weaving Without a Loom*, one by Veronica Burningham (Search Press, 1999) and the other by Sarita Rainey (Davis Publications, 1966) offer a place to begin. The latter is out of print, but I've seen it at my local library and elementary school. It is my favorite of the two as it includes numerous project ideas just for kids as well as expert examples of various techniques. The plus of Burningham's book is its clear, detailed color photographs.

My two favorite books to read to children about the process of turning fiber into fabric are *Charlie Needs a Cloak* (Aladdin Books, 1982) and *A New Coat for Anna* (Dragonfly Books, 1986). Both are excellent, read-aloud books with appealing illustrations.

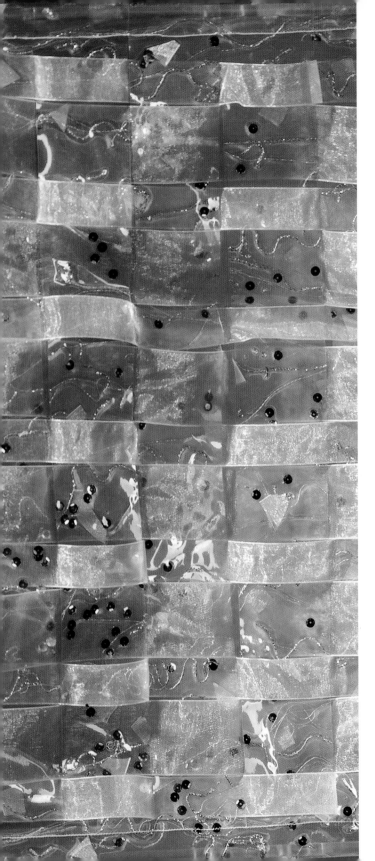

GLOSSARY OF WEAVING TERMS

Balanced weave. Fabric in which the number of warp ends per inch is the same as the number of weft ends per inch.

Beating. When weaving, pressing the weft into place.

Braiding. The process of interlacing threads to make a woven web.

Butterfly. A small bundle of yarn tied into a figure eight and used for weaving.

Discontinuous weft. A weft that does not travel from selvedge to selvedge, but rather several wefts weave short distances to create a pattern, as in tapestry.

Draw in. The tendency of the web to narrow during weaving.

End. One warp yarn (or thread).

E.P.I. (ends per inch). The number of warp ends in one inch.

Fell line. The place on the loom where unwoven warp and web (or woven warp) meet.

Felt. A thick, fuzzy, insulating fabric, usually made of wool.

Felting. The irreversible process of binding fibers together. Usually wool.

Felting needle. A thin, barbed needle used to make felt.

Fiber. The substance, such as wool, from which yarn is spun.

Ghiordes knot. A knot used to make pile. Also called rya knot.

Heddle. A string or metal wire capable of lifting individual warp ends.

Heddle bar. Rod used to hold string heddles. Lifted to raise the heddles to make a shed.

Loom. A frame that holds the warp taut for weaving.

Loom waste. Any yarn that is not woven at the beginning and end of a warp.

Looped pile. A method of making protruding loops by looping weft yarn over a rod, with a plain-weave ground.

Novelty yarn. Generally a fancy, complex yarn that has different twists and irregularities, and fibers.

Pick. One row of weaving.

Pick-up. The technique of holding warps out of the way to create floats in weaving.

Pick-up stick. A narrow stick used to pick up patterns. Also can be turned on edge to form a shed.

Plain weave. The simplest of all weaves, an over, under, over, under interlacement.

Pile. A weft-faced weave with yarns protruding from the surface, often made of knots or loops with a plain-weave ground.

Plaiting. An interlacement in which elements cross each other to form a woven structure, as in braiding and plaited basketry.

Plied yarn. A yarn that is composed of several single strands of yarn twisted together.

P.P.I. (picks per inch). The number of weft rows, or picks, in one inch of weaving.

Selvedge. The edge threads in weaving.

Sett. Number of warp ends in one inch.

Shed. The space between raised and lowered warp threads through which the shuttle passes during weaving.

Shed stick. Narrow stick used to make a shed.

Shuttle. The tool that holds yarn for weaving.

Singles yarn. A yarn made of one strand, not a plied yarn.

Stick shuttle. Flat narrow stick with grooves on the ends used for weaving.

String heddle. Loops made of string to hold warp ends.

Tabby. A plain-weave ground that binds pattern picks.

Tapestry. A weft-faced weave woven of discontinuous wefts.

Twining. A method of twisting two or more weft threads around each other across the warp, often used as the beginning and ending of rugs and constructing baskets.

Warp. The set of threads held taut by a loom.

Warp-faced. Cloth in which only the warp shows.

Warping. The process of putting the warp on the loom.

Weaving. Crossing one set of threads with another. The warps are those threads that are held taut by a loom. The weft is the threads that cross the warp.

Web. On the loom, the warp that has been already woven. Woven fabric.

Weft. The threads that cross the warp.

Weft-faced. Cloth in which only the weft shows.

Yarn. Continous fibers that have been spun or constructed.

RESOURCES

WEAVING AND TEXTILE ART MAGAZINES

Fiberarts
Publisher: Interweave Press LLC
201 East Fourth Street
Loveland, Colorado 80537
www.fiberarts.com

Handwoven
Publisher: Interweave Press LLC
201 East Fourth Street
Loveland, Colorado 80537
www.handwovenmagazine.com

Ornament
Publisher: Ornament Inc.
PO Box 2349
San Marcos, California 92079
www.ornamentmagazine.com

Selvedge
PO Box 40038
London N6 5UW
United Kingdom
www.selvedge.org

Shuttle, Spindle, and Dyepot
Publisher: Handweavers Guild of America
1255 Buford Highway, Suite 211
Suwanee, Georgia 30024
www.weavespindye.org

Surface Design Journal
Publisher: Surface Design Association
PO Box 360
Sebastopol, California 95473
www.surfacedesign.org

Textileforum
Friedenstr 5
PO Box 5944
D-30059 Hannover
Germany
www.ETN-net.org

Väv Magasinet
Westmansgatan 37
SE-582 16 Linkoping
Sweden
www.vavmagasinet.se

WEAVING MANUFACTURERS AND SUPPLIERS USED FOR THIS BOOK

I've used materials and equipment that are easy to find. Yarns and threads such as embroidery floss, 3/2 pearl cotton, and 5/2 pearl cotton are readily available at sewing and craft stores, as well as specialty yarn shops. Look for the following products at specialty yarn stores and mail-order companies that stock weaving tools and supplies. An asterisk (*) indicates a retail mail-order company.

Berroco Inc.
PO Box 367
14 Elmsdale Road
Uxbridge, Massachusetts 01569
www.berroco.com
> *Sizzle Bright* (used in Fuzzy Collar)

Brown Sheep
100662 County Road 16
Mitchell, Nebraska 69357
www.brownsheep.com
> *Lamb's Pride* (used in Pile Patch)

*Cotton Clouds
5176 South 14th Avenue
Safford, Arizona 85546
www.cottonclouds.com
> *3310 Chenille Yarn* (used in Fuzzy Collar)

Crystal Palace
160 23rd Street
Richmond, California 94804
www.straw.com
> *Fling* (used in Fuzzy Collar)

Erdal Yarns Ltd.
2 Forest Avenue
Locust Valley, New York 11560
www.erdal.com
> *Eyelash Tweed* (used in Fuzzy Collar)

Great Northern Weaving/Edgemont Yarns
451 East D Avenue
Kalamazoo, Michigan 49009
www.greatnorthernweaving.com
> *8/4 Carpet Warp* (used in Pile Patch)

*Habu Textiles
135 West 29th Street, Suite 804
New York, New York 10001
www.habutextiles.com
> *Paper Yarn* (used in Tile Wraps)

Harrisville Designs
Box 806
41 Main Street
Harrisville, New Hampshire 03450
www.harrisville.com
> *Highland 2-ply Wool* (used in Pocket Purse)
> *Peg Loom* (used in Pocket Purse)
> *Shetland 2-ply Wool* (used in Egg Hat)

Schacht Spindle Company Inc.
6101 Ben Place
Boulder, Colorado 80301
www.schachtspindle.com
> *Schacht Mini Loom* (used in Pile Patch)
> *Schacht School Loom* (used in Egg Hat)

BIBLIOGRAPHY

BAMBOO

Austin, Robert, and Ueda Koichiro. *Bamboo.* New York: John Weatherhill Inc., 1975.

Strangler, Carol. *The Craft and Art of Bamboo.* New York: Lark Books, Sterling Publishing, 2001.

BASKETRY

Daugherty, Robin Taylor. *Splint Woven Basketry.* New York: Sterling Publishing, 1999.

Harvey, Virginia I. *The Techniques of Basketry.* Seattle, Washington: University of Washington Press, 1986.

Hoppe, Flo. *Wicker Basketry.* Loveland, Colorado: Interweave Press, 1989.

Jensen, Elizabeth. *Baskets from Nature's Bounty.* Loveland, Colorado: Interweave Press, 1991.

LaFerla, Jane. *Making the New Baskets.* Asheville, North Carolina: Lark Books, 1999.

LaPlantz, Shereen. *Plaited Basketry: The Woven Form.* Bayside, California: Press de LaPlantz, 1982.

BEADS

Bateman, Sharon. *Findings and Finishings.* Loveland, Colorado: Interweave Press, 2003.

Benson, Ann. *Beadweaving: New Needle Techniques & Original Designs.* New York: Sterling Publishing, 1993.

Campbell, Jean, and Judith Durant. *The Beader's Companion.* Loveland, Colorado: Interweave Press, 1998, 2006.

Clarke, Amy C., and Robin Atkins. *Beaded Embellishment: Techniques & Designs for Embroidering on Cloth.* Loveland, Colorado: Interweave Press, 2002.

Coles, Janet, and Robert Budwig. *The Book of Beads.* New York: Simon and Schuster, 1990.

COLOR

Itten, Johannes. *The Elements of Color.* New York: Van Nostrand Reinhold, 1970.

Menz, Deb. *Color Works.* Loveland, Colorado: Interweave Press, 2004.

Stockton, James. *Designer's Guide to Color.* San Francisco: Chronicle Books, 1984.

COLOR-AND-WEAVE

Sutton, Ann. *Colour-and-Weave Design Book: A Practical Reference Book*. Asheville, North Carolina: Lark Books, 1984.

————. *Ideas in Weaving*. Asheville, North Carolina: Lark Books, 1982.

FELTING

Docherty, Margaret, and Jayne Emerson. *Simply Felt*. Loveland, Colorado: Interweave Press, 2004.

Galeskas, Beverly. *Felted Knits*. Loveland, Colorado: Interweave Press, 2003.

Gordon, Beverly. *Feltmaking: Traditions, Techniques, and Contemporary Explorations*. New York: Watson-Guptill Publications, 1980.

Hagen, Chad Alice. *The Weekend Crafter: Feltmaking: Fabulous Wearable Jewelry, and Home Accents*. Asheville, North Carolina: Lark Books, 2002.

Mavor, Salley. *Felt Wee Folk: Enchanting Projects*. Lafayette, California: C&T Publishing, 2003.

Sjoberg, Gunilla Paetau, trans. Patricia Spark. *Felt: New Directions for an Ancient Craft*. Loveland, Colorado: Interweave Press, 1996.

Vickrey, Anne Einset. *The Art of Feltmaking*. New York: Watson-Guptill Publications, 1997.

FOLK TRADITIONS

Collingwood, Peter. *The Maker's Hand*. Loveland, Colorado: Interweave Press, 1987.

Hideyuki Oka. *How to Wrap Five Eggs*. New York: Harper and Row, 1967.

Sekijima, Hisako. *Basketry Projects from Baskets to Grass Slippers*. New York: Kodansha International, 1986.

KNOTS AND BRAIDING

Ashley, Clifford. *The Ashley Book of Knots*. Reissue edition. New York: Doubleday, 1944.

Baizerman, Suzanne, and Karen Searle. *Finishes in the Ethnic Tradition*. St. Paul, Minnesota: Dos Tejedoras, 1978.

Budworth, Geoffrey. *The Complete Book of Decorative Knots*. New York: Lyons Press, 1998.

Owen, Peter. *The Book of Decorative Knots*. New York: Lyons and Burford, 1994.

Owen, Rodrick. *Braids: 250 Patterns from Japan, Peru, and Beyond*. Loveland, Colorado: Interweave Press, 1995.

————. *Making Kumihimo: Japanese Interlaced Braids*. Lewes, United Kingdom: Guild of Master Craftsman Publications, 2004.

Pawson Des. *The Handbook of Knots*. New York: DK Publishing, 1998.

Shaw, George Russell, *Knots: Useful and Ornamental*. New York: McMillan Publishers, 1972.

PAPER AND LAMP MAKING

Asuncion, Josep. *The Complete Book of Papermaking*. London: Batsford, 2003.

Cusick, Dawn. *The Lamp Shade Book*. New York: Lark Books, Sterling Publishing, 1996.

Driscoll, Maryellen. *The Paper Shade Book*. Gloucester, Massachusetts: Rockport Publishers, 2001.

Heller, Jules. *Paper-Making*. New York: Watson-Guptill Publications, 1978.

Morgenthal, Deborah. *Making Great Lamps: 50 Illuminating Projects, Techniques, and Ideas*. Asheville, North Carolina: Lark Books, 1998.

Turner, Silvie. *The Book of Fine Paper*. New York: Thames and Hudson Inc., 1998.

TEXTILE DESIGN

Aimone, Katherine Duncan. *The Fiberarts Book of Wearable Art*. Asheville, North Carolina: Lark Books, 2002.

Braddock, Sarah E., and Marie O'Mahony. *Techno Textiles*. New York: Thames and Hudson, 2001.

Koumis, Matthew, ed. *Art Textiles of the World: USA Vol.1*. Winchester, England: Telos Art Publishing, 2000.

Takekura, Masaaki, publisher. *Suke Suke*. Tokyo, Japan: Nuno Corporation, 1997.

WEAVING

Alderman, Sharon. *Mastering Weave Structures*. Loveland, Colorado: Interweave Press, 2004.

Atwater, Mary Meigs. *Byways in Handweaving: An Illustrated Guide to Rare Weaving Techniques*. Coupeville, Washington: Shuttlecraft Books, 1992, distributed by Unicorn Books.

Chandler, Deborah. *Learning to Weave*, revised edition. Loveland Colorado: Interweave Press, 1995.

Collingwood, Peter. *The Techniques of Rug Weaving*. New York: Watson-Guptill Publications, 1972.

Held, Shirley. *Weaving: A Handbook for Fiber Craftsmen*. New York: Holt Rinehart and Winston, 1973.

Irwin, Bobbie. *Twined Rag Rugs: Traditions in the Making.* Iola, Wisconsin: Krause Publications, 2000.

Redman, Jane. *Frame-Loom Weaving.* New York: Van Nostrand Reinhold, 1976.

Sutton, Ann. *Colour-and-Weave Design: A Practical Reference Book.* Asheville, North Carolina: Lark Books, 1984.

———. *The Structure of Weaving.* Asheville, North Carolina: Lark Books, 1982.

Van der Hoogt, Madelyn. *Weaver's Companion.* Loveland, Colorado: Interweave Press, 2001.

WEAVING FOR KIDS

Burningham, Veronica. *Weaving Without a Loom.* Turnbridge Wells, Kent, England: Search Press, 1999.

DePaola, Tomie. *Charlie Needs a Cloak.* New York: Aladdin Books, 1982.

Rainey, Sarita R. *Weaving Without a Loom.* Worchester, Massachusetts: Davis Publications, 1966.

Ziefert, Harriet. *A New Coat for Anna.* New York: Alfred Knopf, Dragonfly Books, 1986.

INDEX